AF375235

Lemuel Parker, Bingham Photographer

Compiled by Rick Warwick
Williamson County Historian

Edited by Marcia P. Fraser, Special Collections Librarian
Williamson County Public Library

A Publication of Williamson County Historical Society
2022

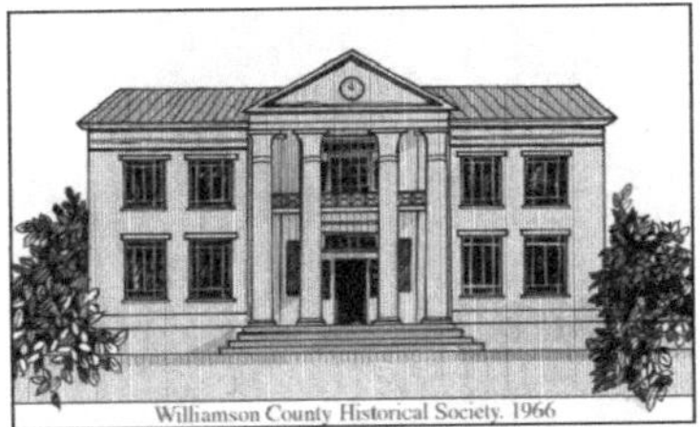

Library of Congress Control Number: 2022909830
ISBN: 979-8-9863055-0-9

Introduction

While working on *Out There in the First District,* in 2001, Pepper Bruce of the Fernvale community brought me a box of photographic glass plates given to him by Dr. Walter Pyle in 1961. Dr. Pyle had purchased the Lemuel Parker farm on Parker Branch Road in 1955 and found the box in the attic of the Parker log-farm house. Apparently, Lemuel Parker had taken up photography around 1911 and left us with a magnificent photographic documentary of the Leiper's Fork and Bingham communities from 1911 to 1921. What a wonderful legacy Mr. Parker left behind.

The Williamson County Historical Society takes great pleasure in making these marvelous glimpses into the second decade of the 20th century available. These views of the local folk, their homes, churches, schools, and village of Leiper's Fork are priceless. I hope you enjoy them as much as I have.

Rick Warwick,
President of the Williamson County Historical Society
and Williamson County Historian

Lemuel Parker, Bingham Photographer

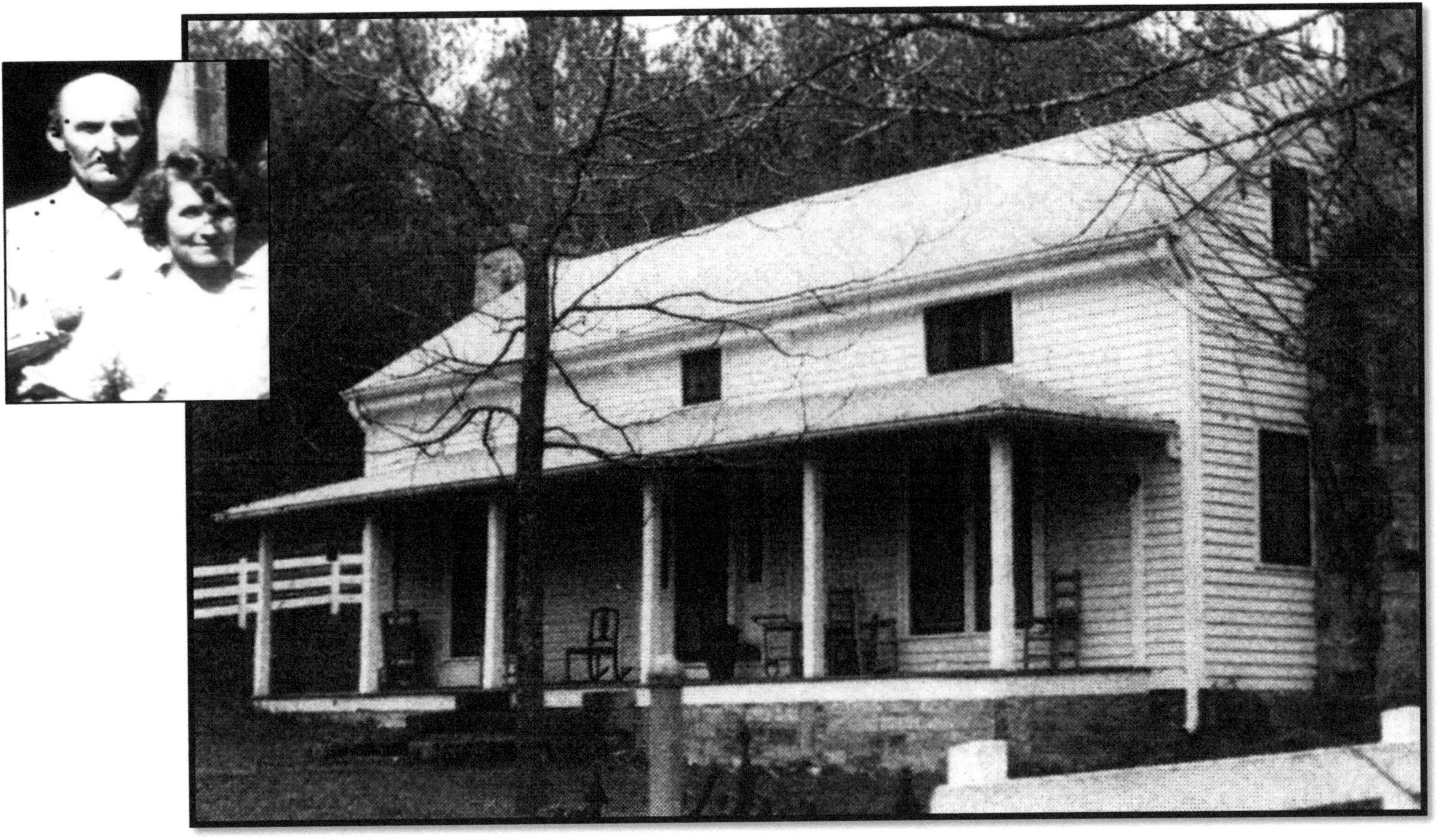

The home of Lemuel and Laura McPherson Parker on Parker Branch Road, built by his grandfather, W. J. Bingham, in 1865. The photographic glass plates were found upstairs in a corner.

Lemuel and Laura McPherson and Sons

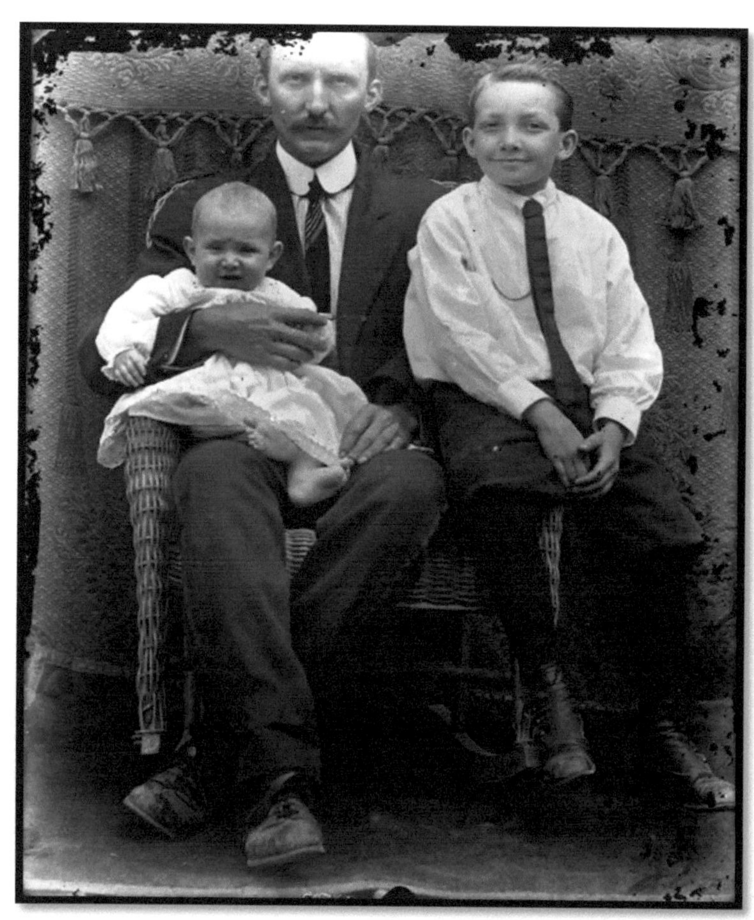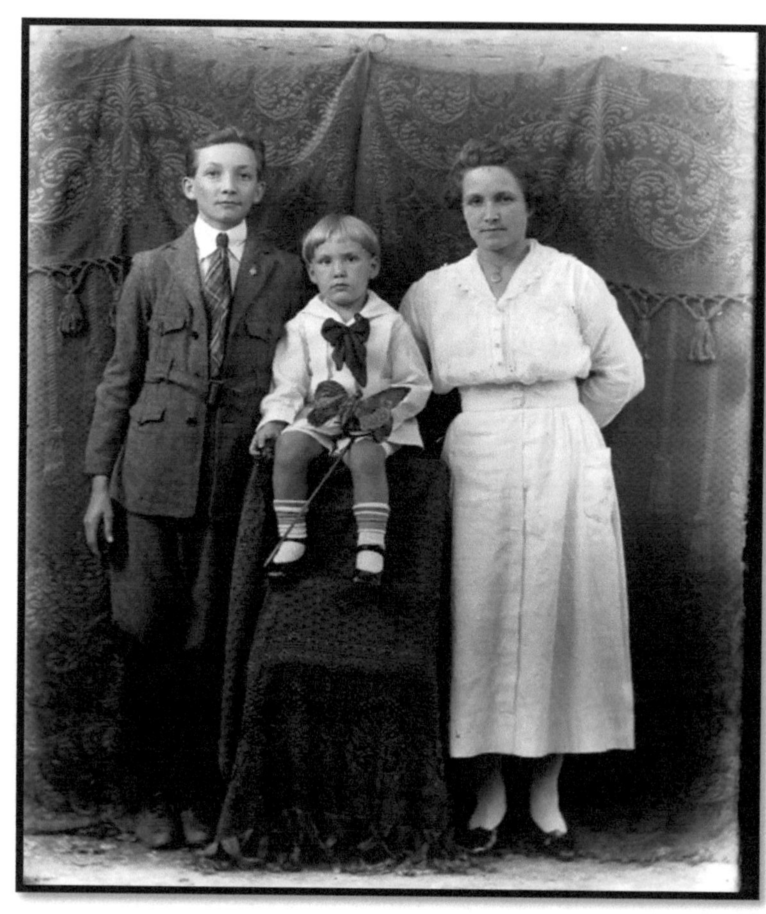

Lemuel Parker (1879-1956) married Laura McPherson Parker (1888-1969) in 1904. They became the parents of Millard Clinton Parker (1906-unknown) and Harley Eddleman Parker (1916-1973). Lemuel began photography around 1911.

Laura Parker with Millard and Harley

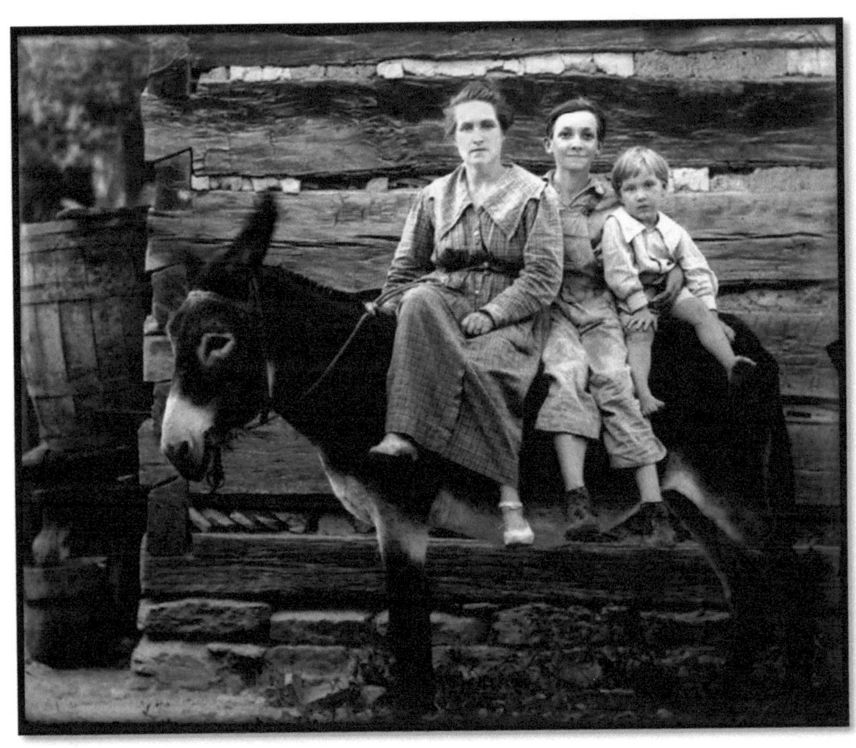

Lemuel Parker took these photographs around 1918, of wife, Laura, and sons, Millard and Harley, in front of the log smokehouse in back of their home.

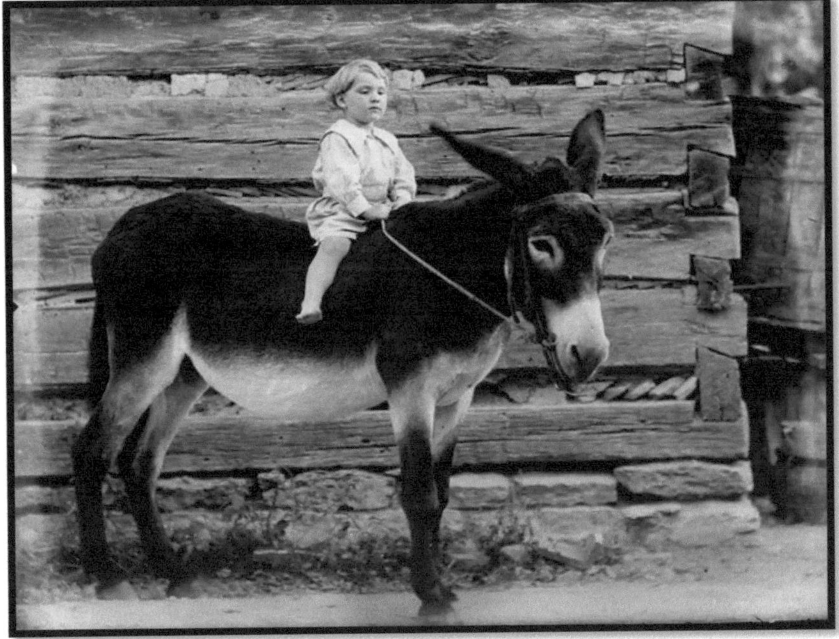

Parents and In-Laws of Lemuel and Laura Parker

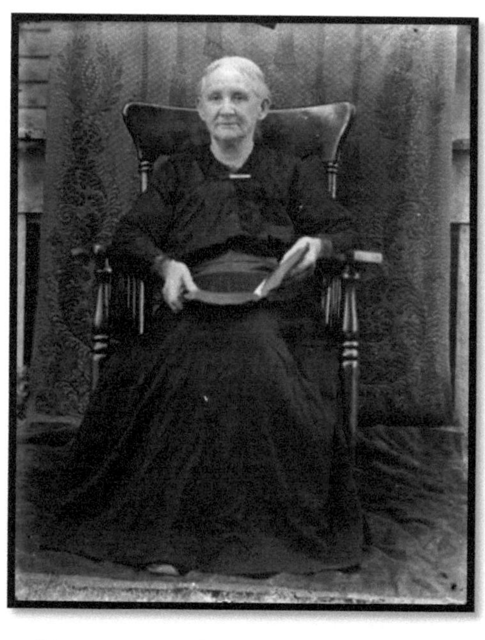

Amanda Bingham Parker
⟵ (1841-1927)

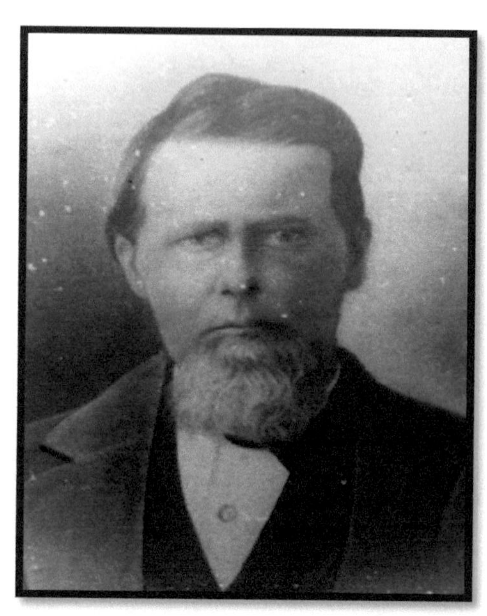

DeWitt Clinton Parker
(1831-1908) ⟶
CSA veteran and
Williamson County Court Clerk

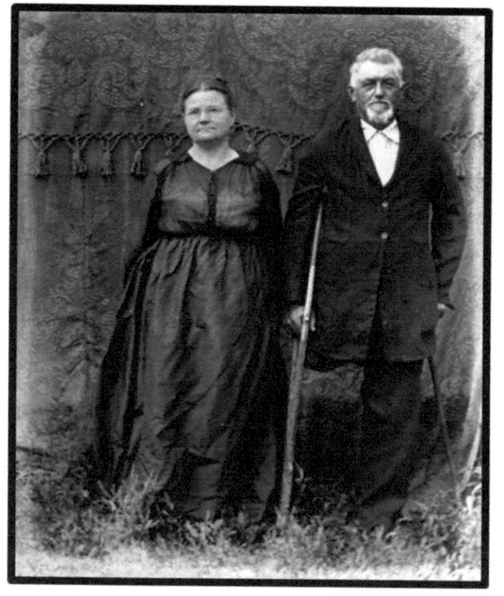

Bettie Forehand McPherson
⟵ (1861-1936), and
John B. McPherson
(1855-1933)
and daughters ⟶
Florence Caldwell,
Bessie White, Laura Parker,
and Lula Mai Ferguson

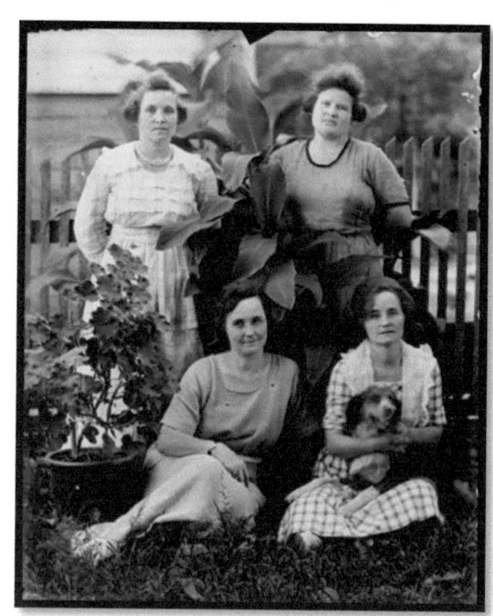

A Visit to Fernvale Springs on July 4, 1916

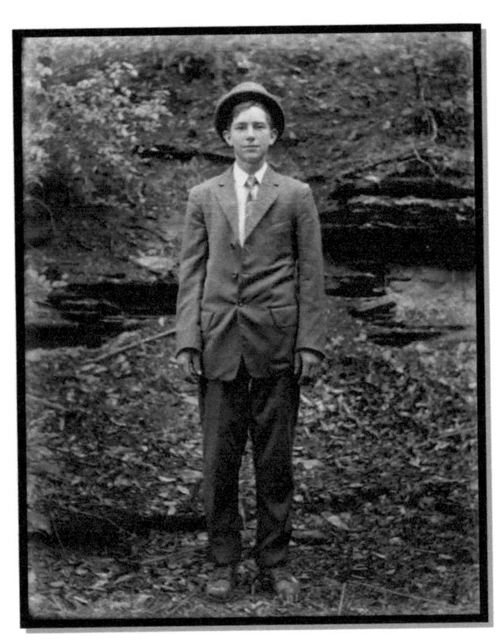

Friend, John Henry Givens

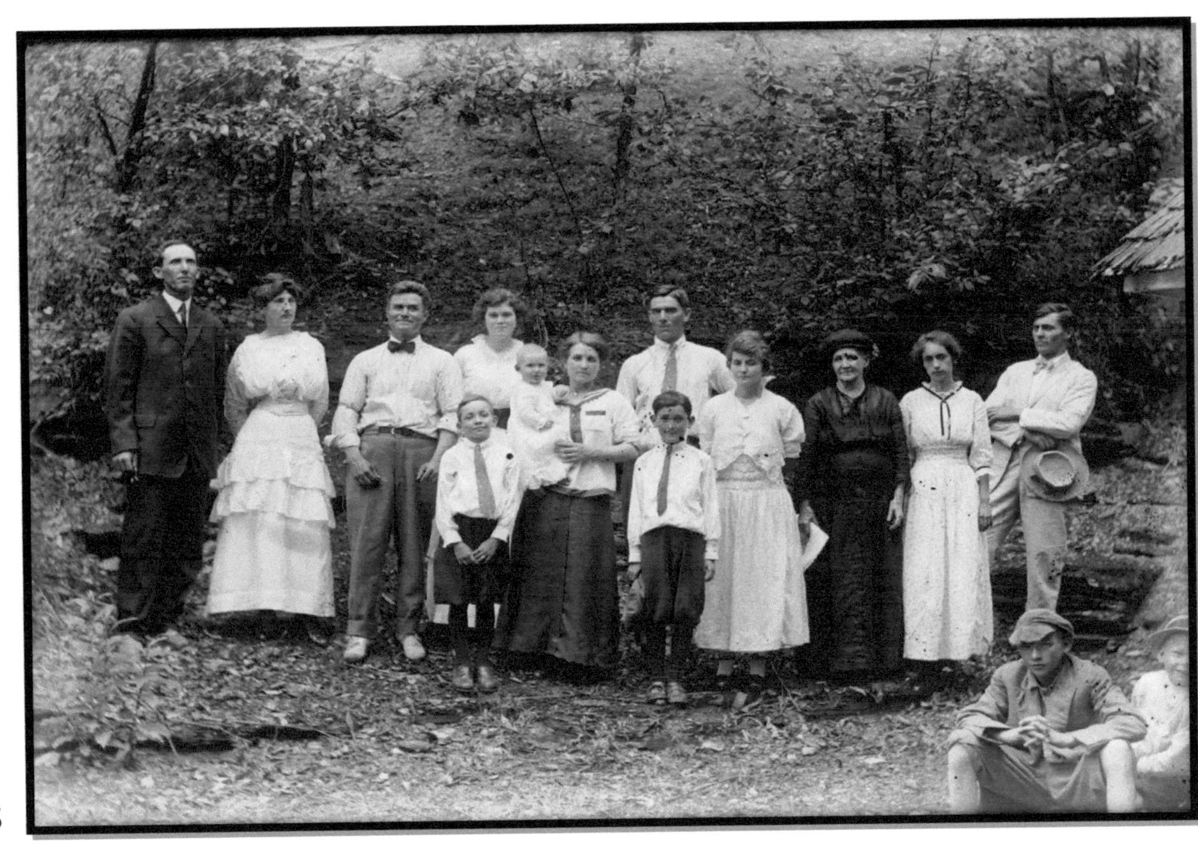

Brother John Parker and his wife, Sadie Pentacost; brother-in-law, Green McPherson and his wife, Jennie Grimes; Millard, Baby Harley, Laura Parker, unidentified boy and man; sister-in-law, Bessie McPherson and mother, Amanda Parker.

The rest are unknown.

Bingham Neighbors and Cousins

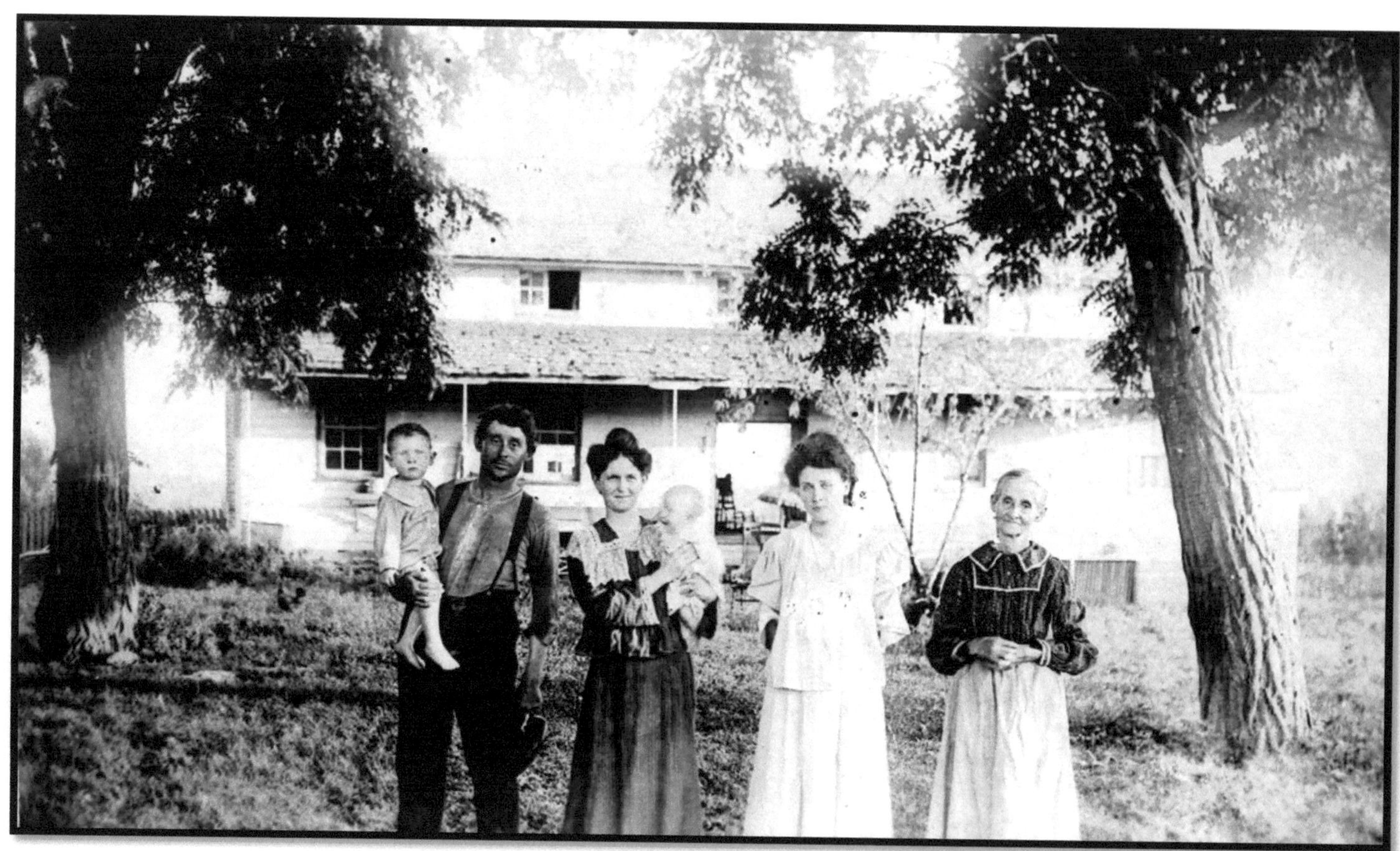

The Robert Poynor family at Dr. A. B. Poynor's home. Robert and Lemuel were first cousins. Robert Poynor, holding Willard; wife, Susie Pewitt holding her niece, Marion; Bernice Cato, mother; and Millie Bingham Poynor.

Horse and Buggy Days

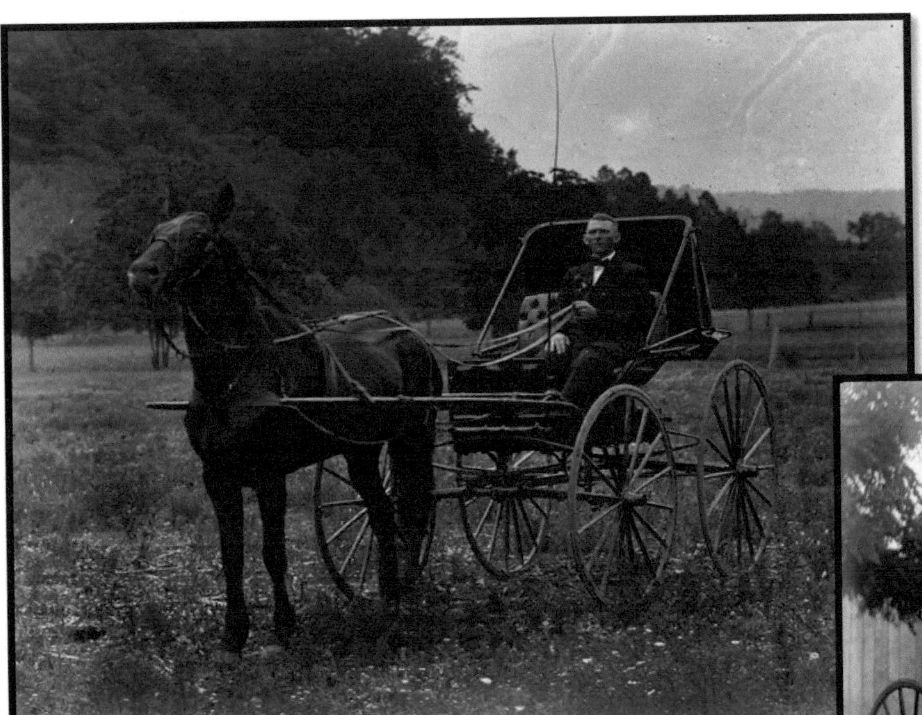

Neighbor Church Hooten
poses in horse and buggy.

Unidentified neighbors pose
for Lemuel Parker's camera.

The Tin Lizzy comes to Bingham

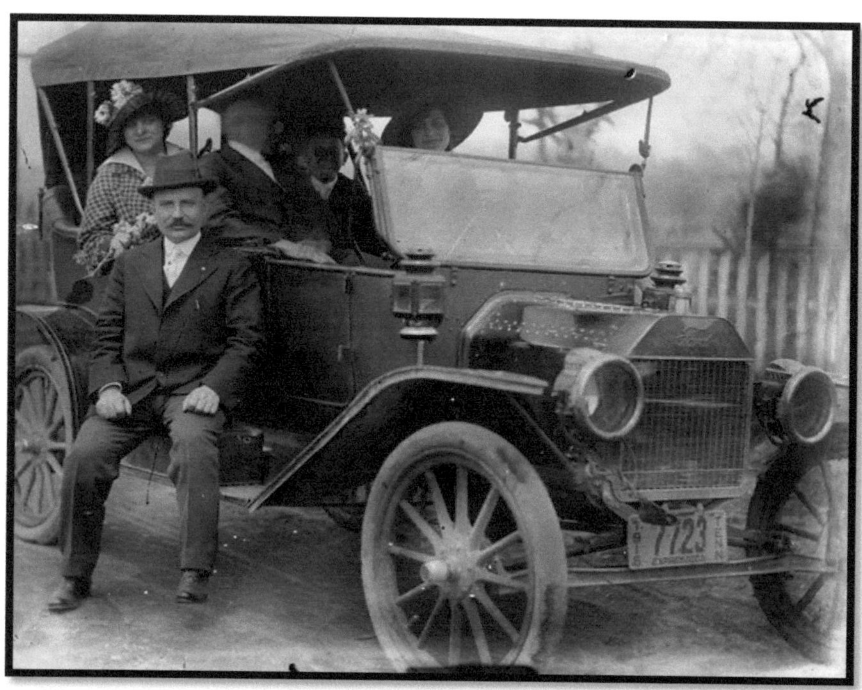

Dr. Harley Eddleman and family of Leiper's Fork and their Ford with 1916 license plate.

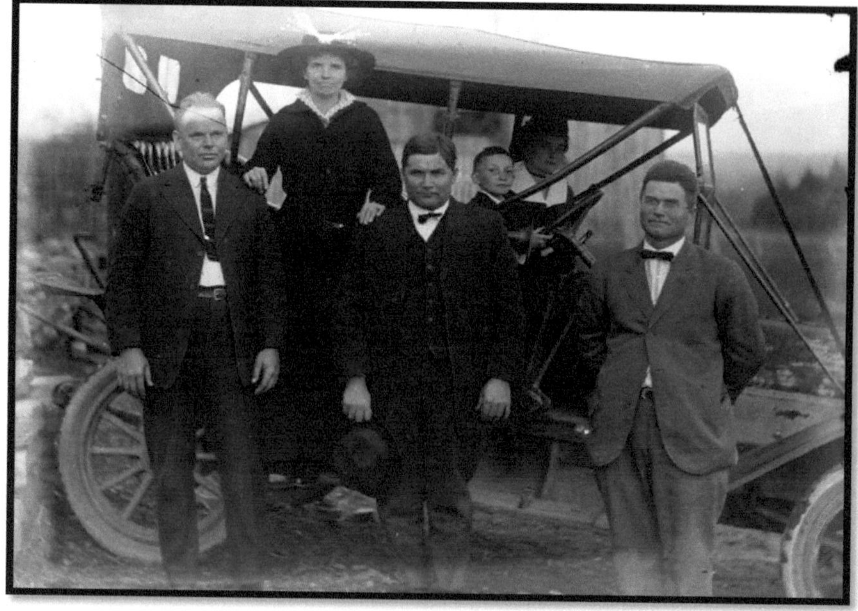

Unidentified couple on left, brothers-in-law Robert and Green McPherson, son Millard and wife Laura in car.

West Harpeth Cumberland Presbyterian Church — Hog-Eye

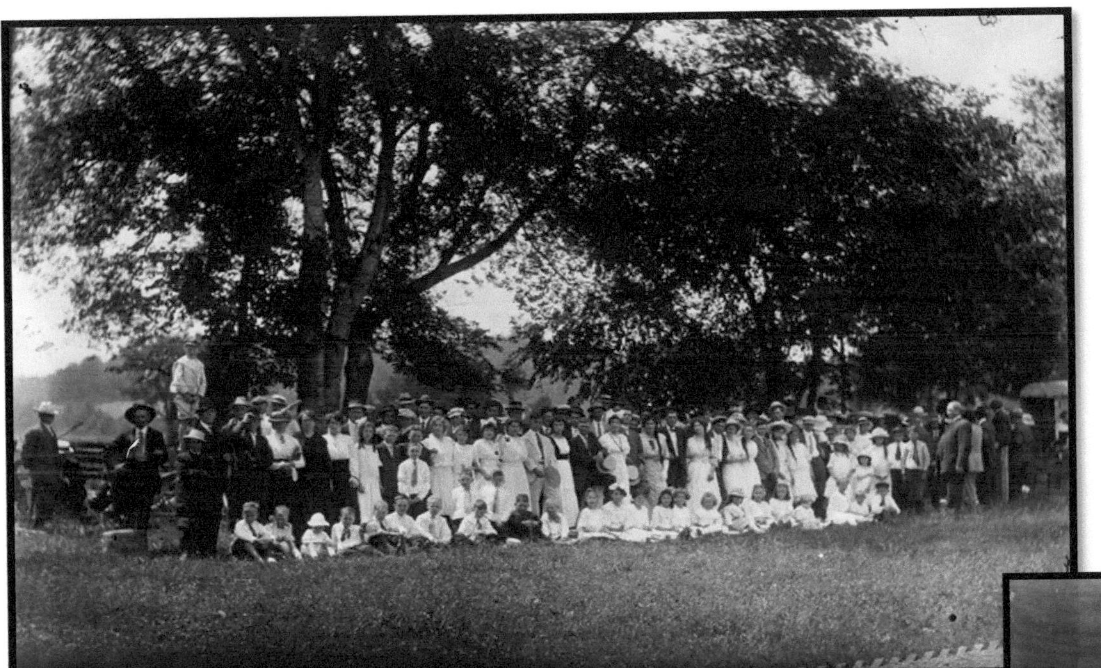

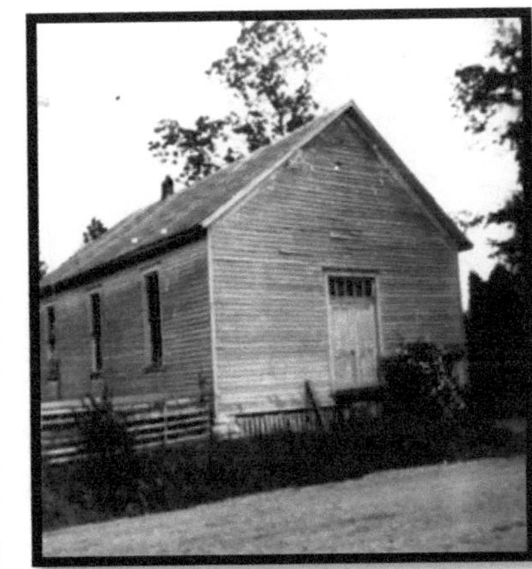

Hog-Eye Church burned in 1976.

Hog-Eye Church was located on Old Hillsboro Road at the intersection of Parker Branch Road.

Singing School Class is seen on the right.
ca. 1918

Hog Killing Time on Parker Branch

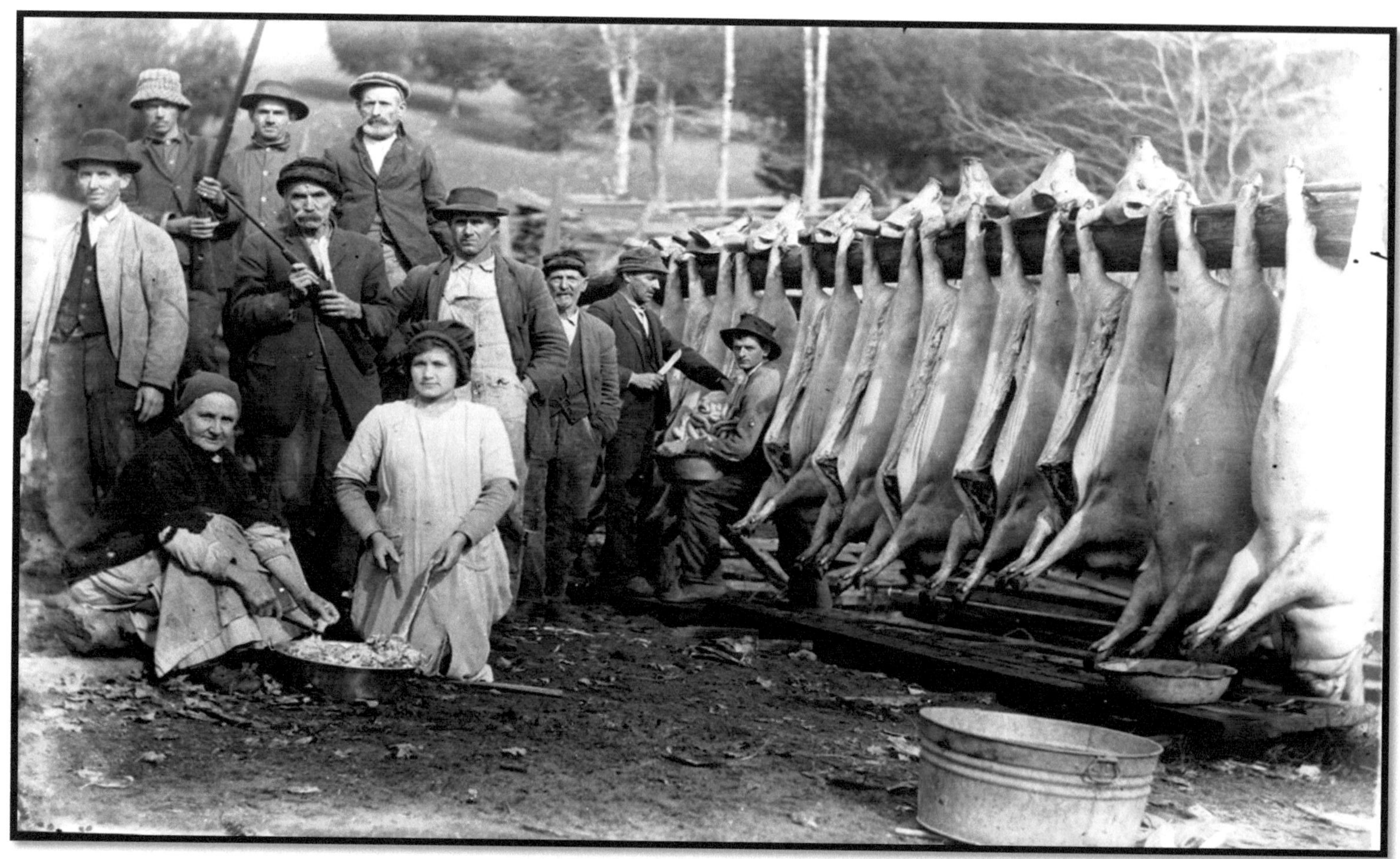

Mother, Amanda Parker, and wife, Laura Parker, are cleaning chitterlings with Bingham neighbors. The young man on the back row is holding a rifle made by W. J. Kirby of Fernvale.

Bingham School

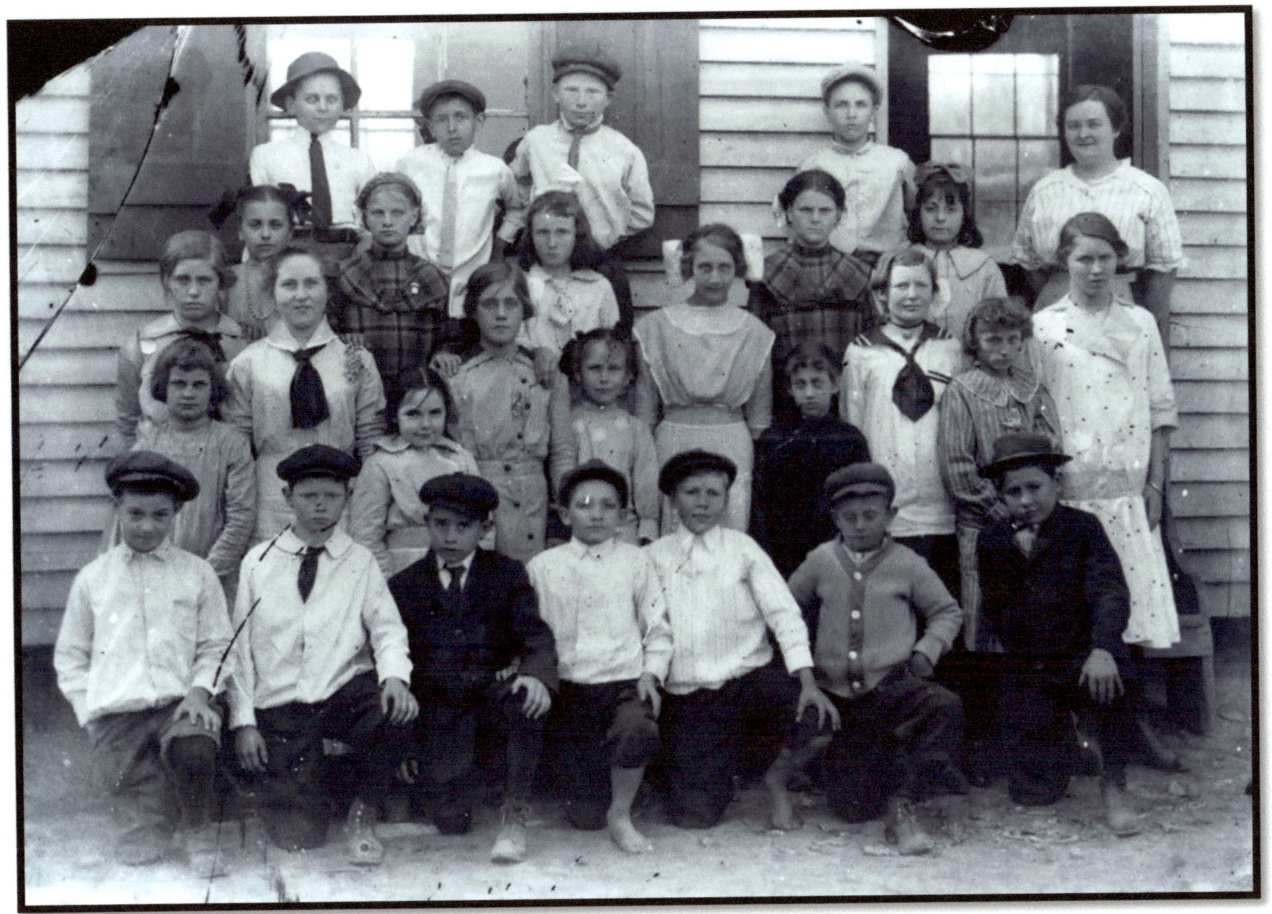

Bingham School ca. 1911 - Miss Essie Cotton, Teacher

1st row: Claude Forehand, Nathan Wiltshire, Powell Boyd, Millard Parker, Frank Owen, Connie Pruett, Herman Sawyer.

2nd row: Maggie Meacham, Kate Akin, _______ Boxley, Elberta Sawyer, Margherita Meacham, Benita Rader, Elna Morton, Sue Owen, Ellen Moore, Addie Forehand.

3rd row: Ethel Sawyer, Florence Meacham, Hattie Meacham, Hazel Blankenship, Mattie Meacham, Bertha Moore.

4th row: Dan Chapman, Charlie Morton, Bennet Blankenship, Turner Meacham, Miss Essie Cotton.

Next-Door Neighbors - Daughters of John Meacham

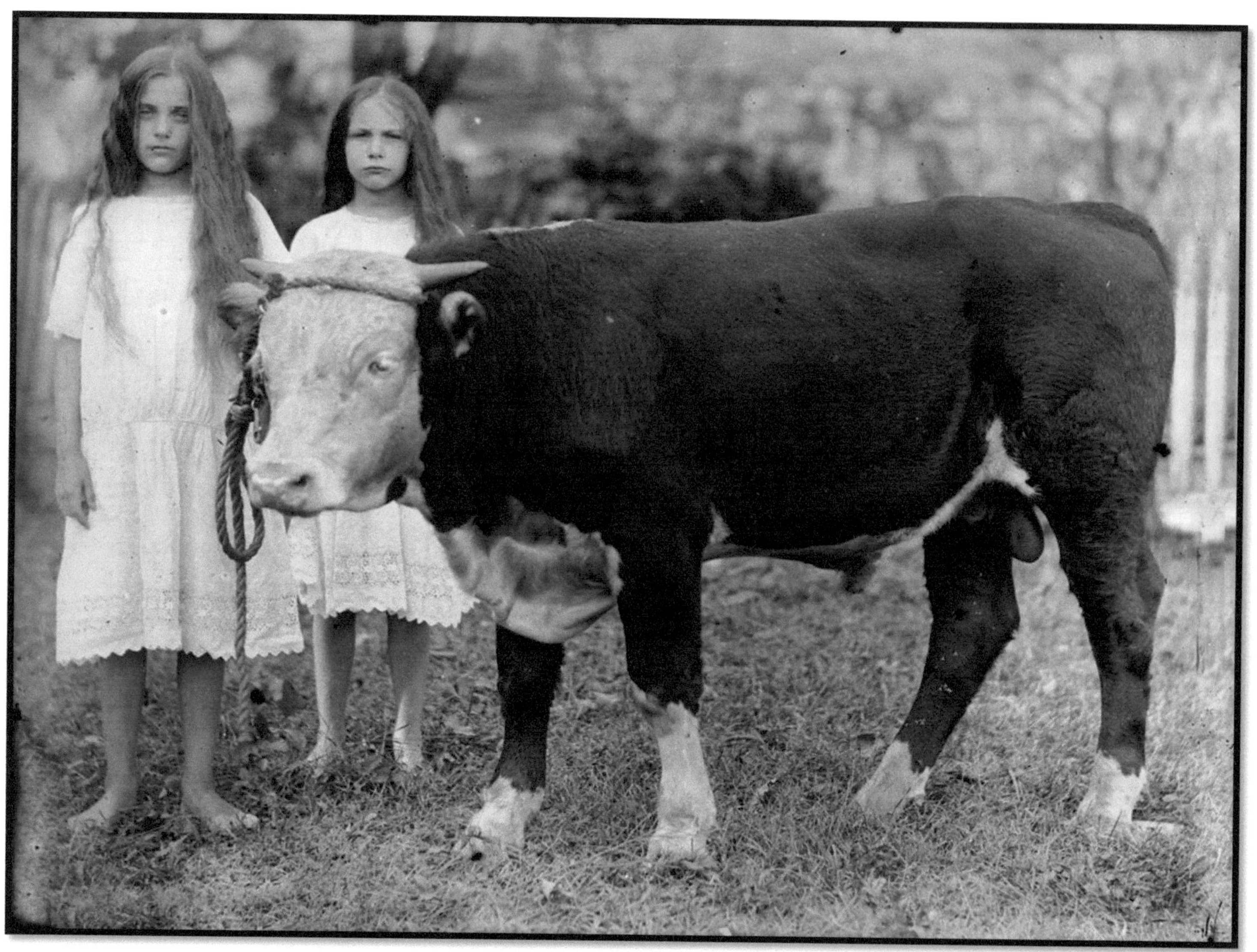

Florence and Margherita Meacham with Hereford bull. ca. 1914

Boyd's Mill on the West Harpeth River

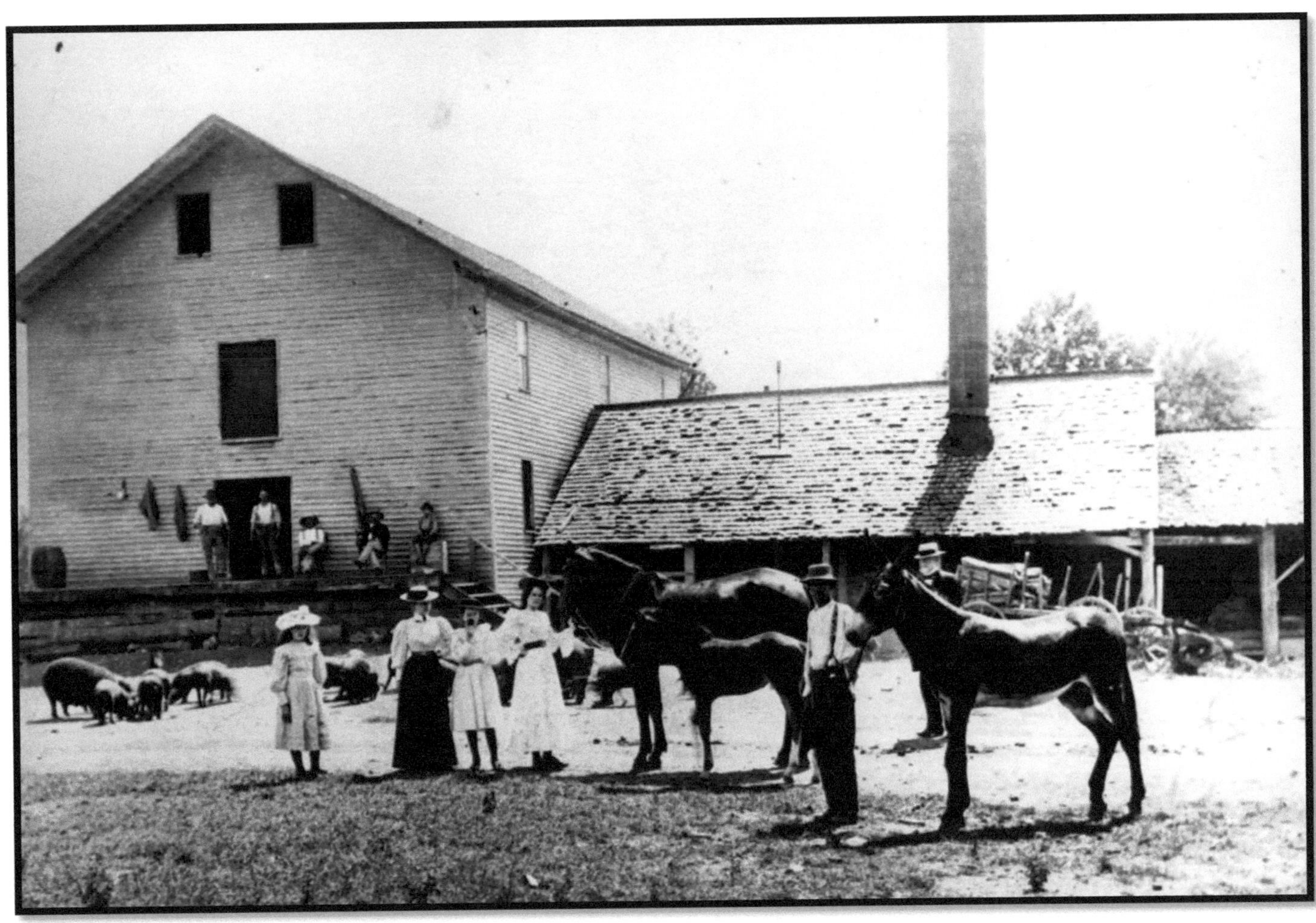

Boyd's Mill, on the West Harpeth River, was the social and economic center of the Bingham community. It produced corn meal and wheat flour using waterpower whenever possible and steam-power when the river was low.

A Bucolic View of the J. E. Boyd Farm

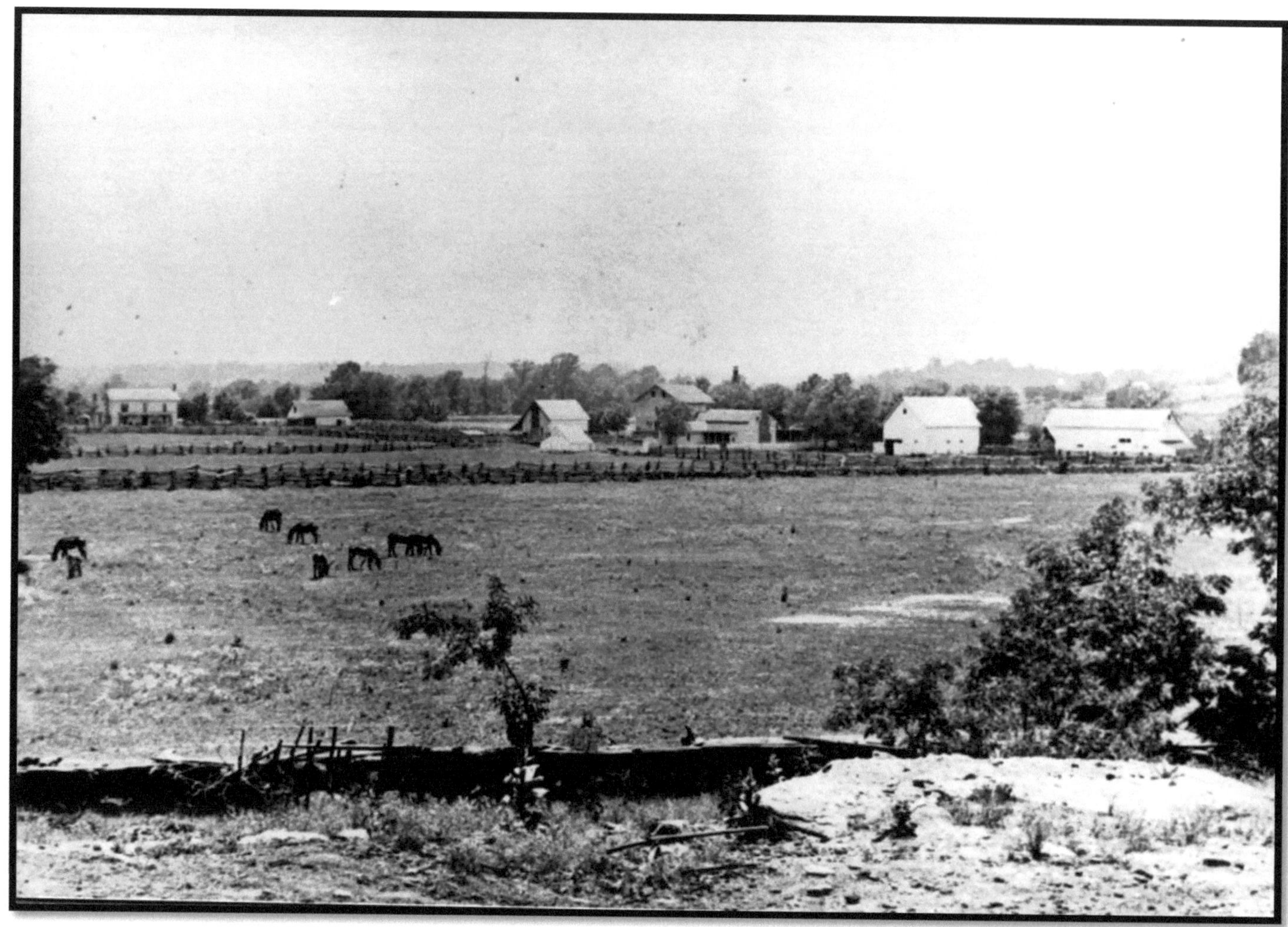

This panoramic view of the John E. Boyd farm shows the two-story house, the grist mill, mule barn, hay barns and the miller's house. Lem Parker captured this view from the W. A. Boyd farm, which overlooks one of the most bucolic rural scenes on the West Harpeth.

Bingham Landmarks

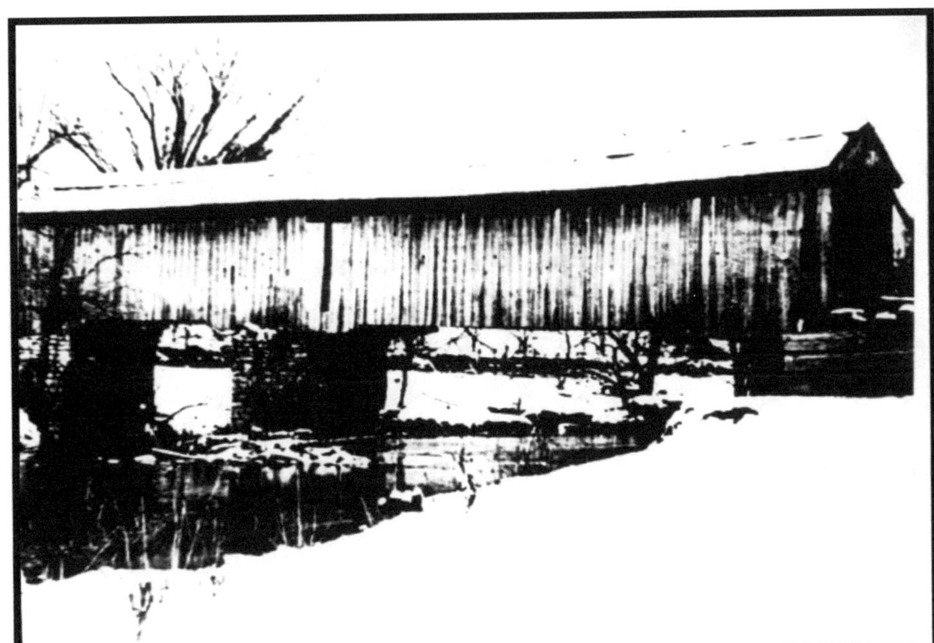

The Bingham covered bridge over the West Harpeth River was built in 1878 and was replaced with an iron bridge in 1929.

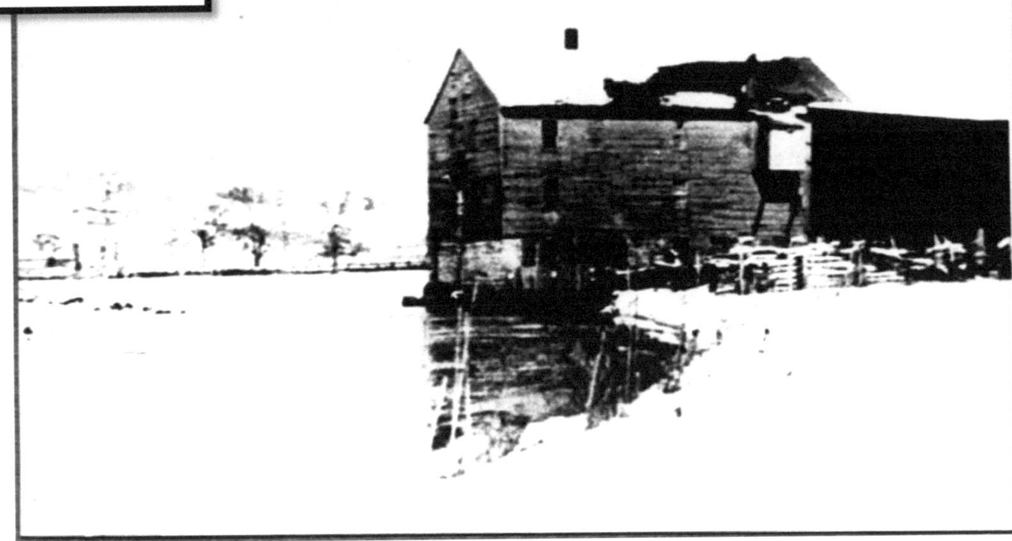

Stone's Mill was located here as early as 1813 and became Boyd's Mill after the Civil War. The mill was powered by water and a steam engine during low water. It ceased to operate in 1917. The stone foundation can still be seen.

Votes for Women

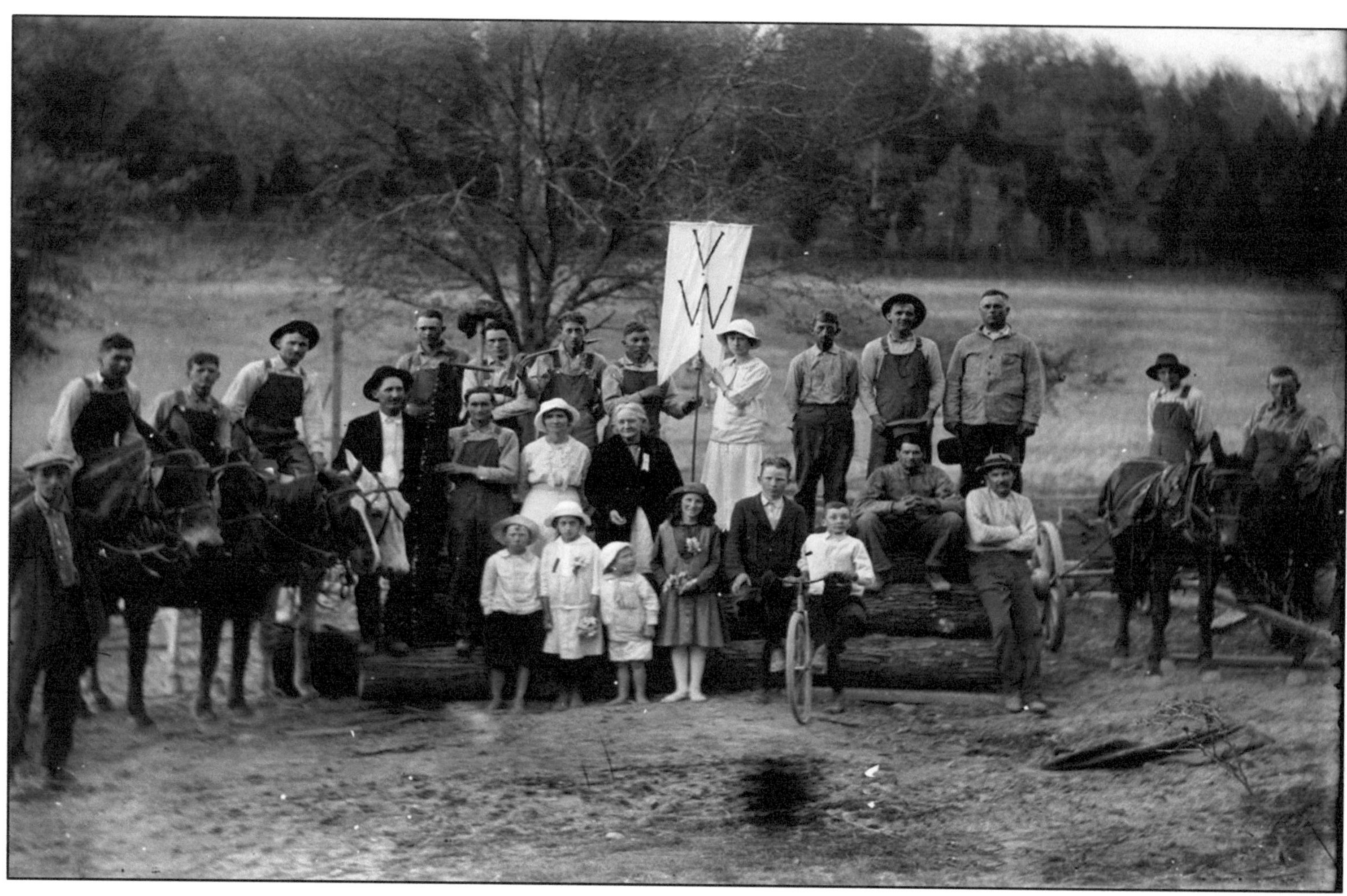

On October 5, 1918, Franklin had a Liberty Bond Parade and the Votes for Women committee took part in the parade. Bonnie Blankenship holds the banner used in the parade with the initials VW. This photograph was taken at Lemuel Parker's sawmill.

Bingham Neighbors

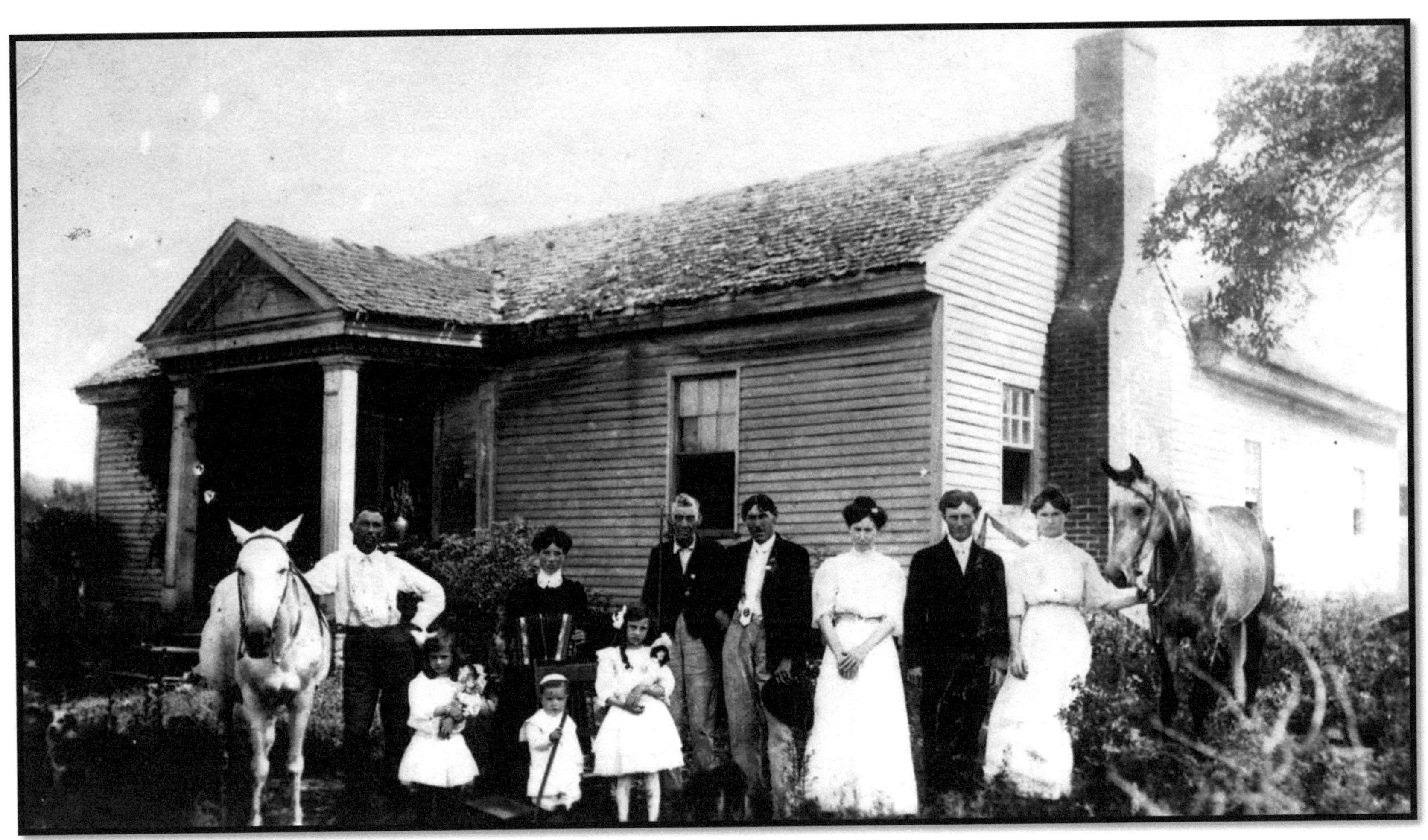

The Charlie Boyd home and family on Boyd Mill Pike

Joe and May Poynor Blankenship of Waddell Hollow

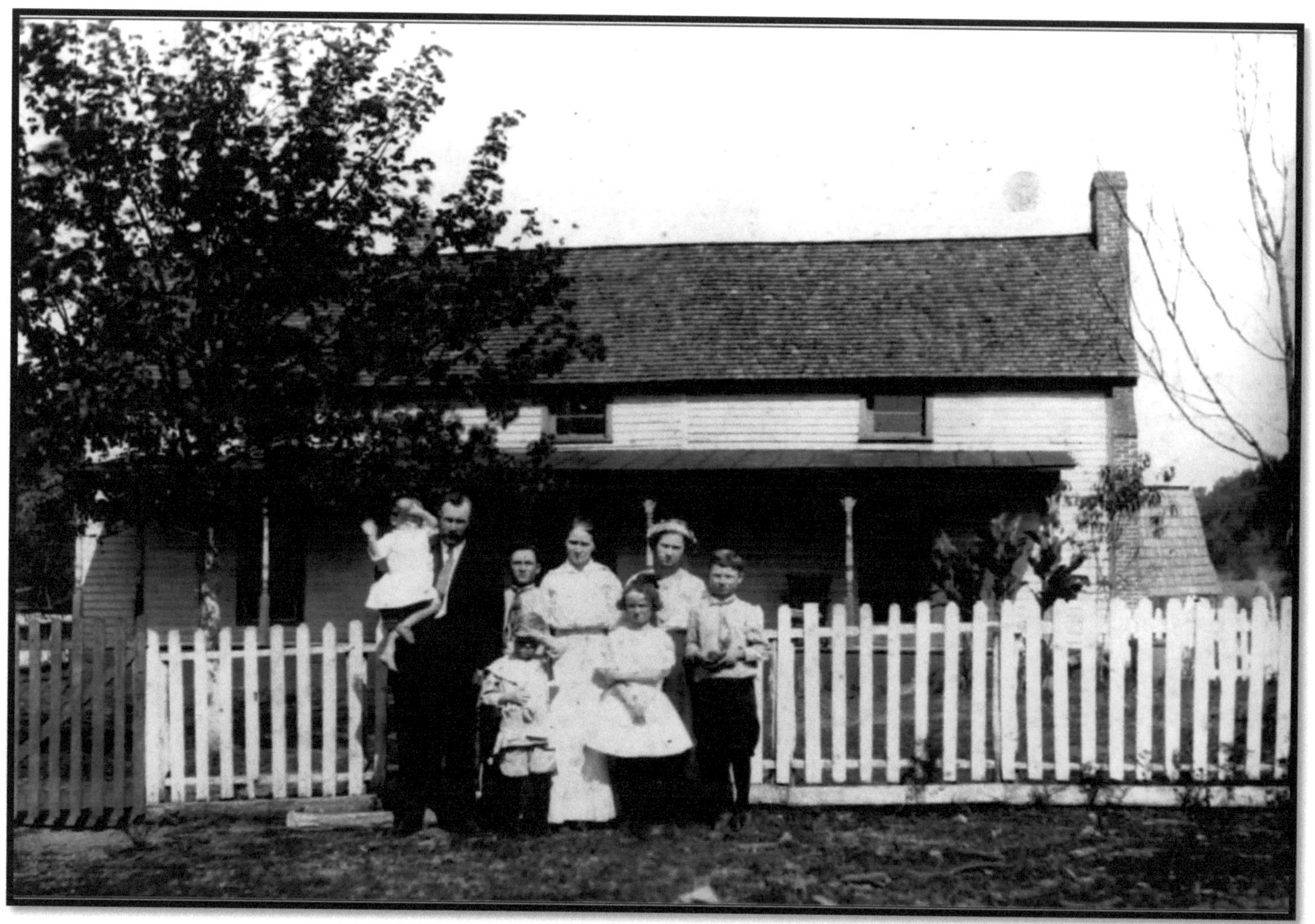

The Joe Blankenship family lived in Waddell Hollow. Joe was the blacksmith for the Bingham community, whose shop was located next to Short's Store on Old Hillsboro Road. May was the daughter of Dr. A. B. Poynor and a first cousin to Lem Parker.

Waddell Hollow Neighbors

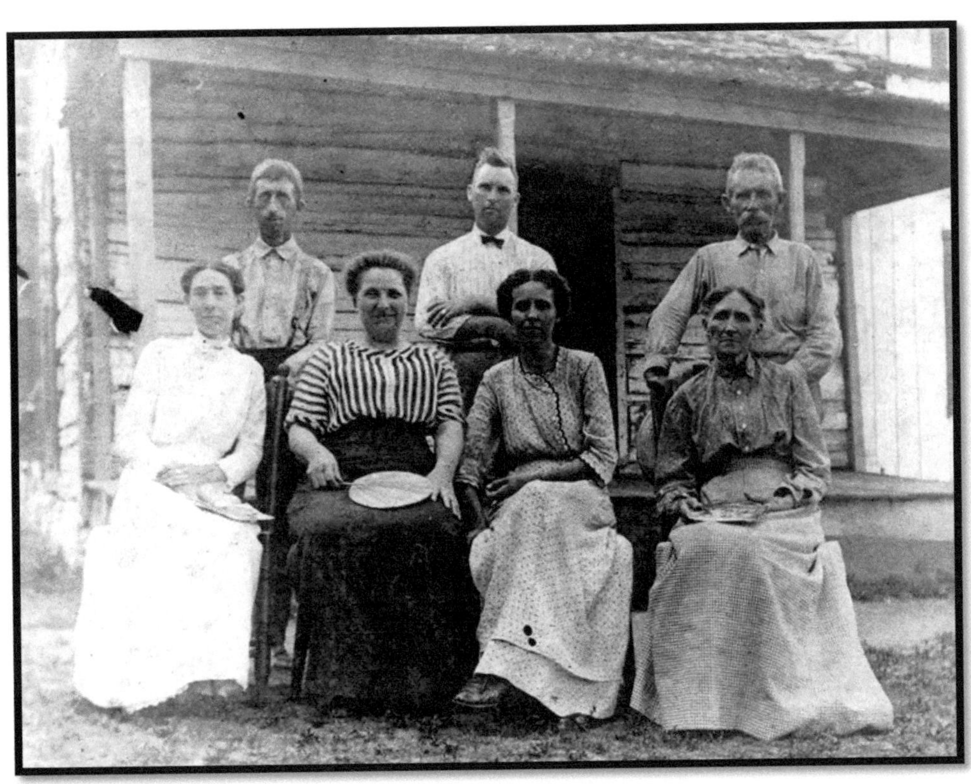

Nellie Waddell Garrett, Mag Waddell, Addie Waddell, Kate Cox Waddell, Dee Garrett, Miller Garrett, and W. S. Waddell.

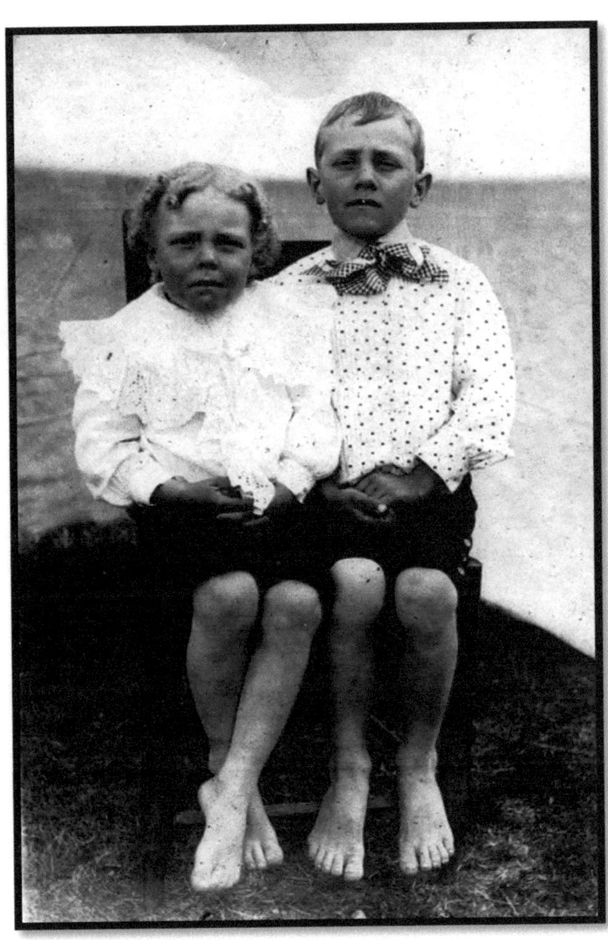

Luther and Leland Waddell

Kingfield Neighbors

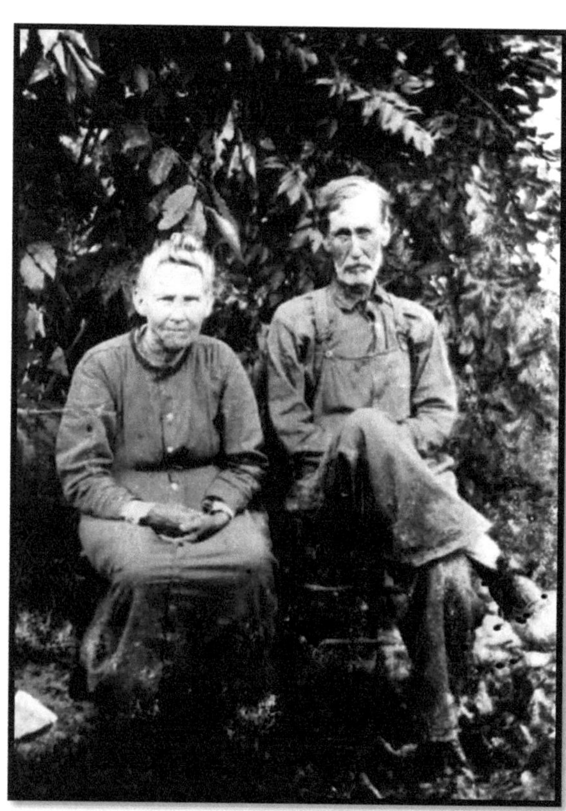

Sophronia Howell and
Solomon King

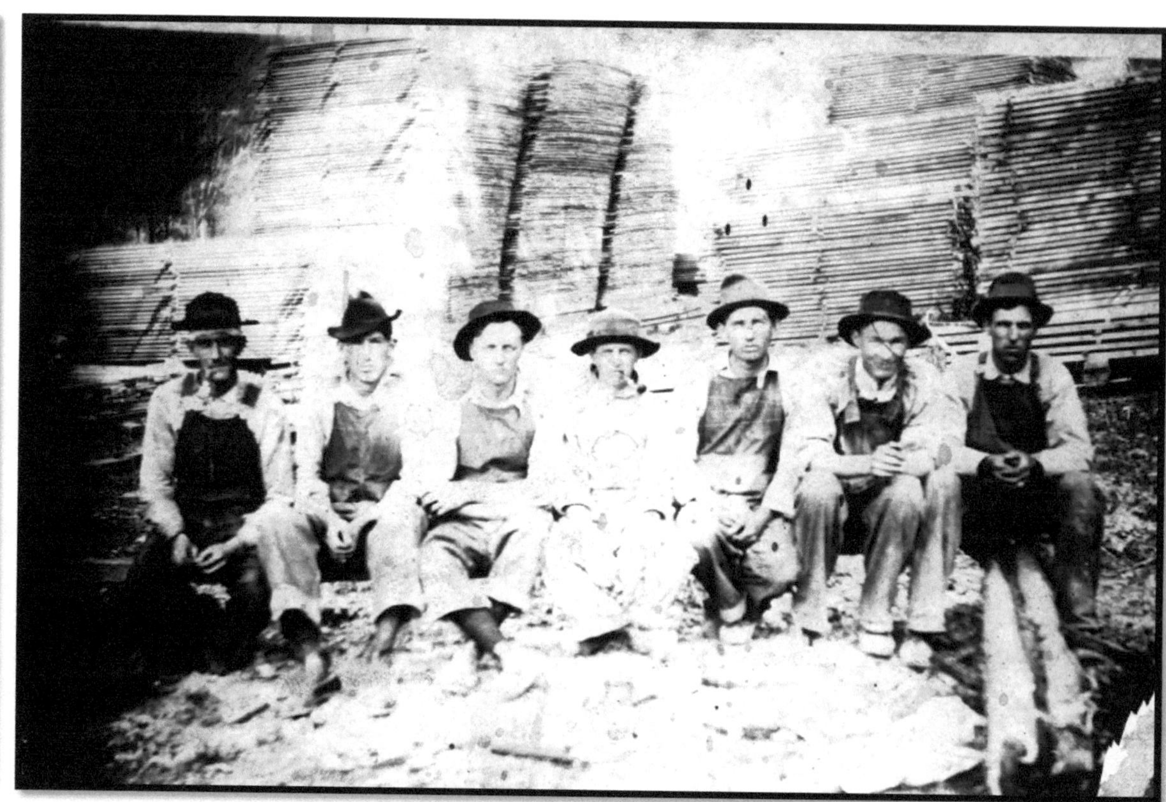

Southall Brothers' Sawmill hands:
Kings, Howells, Inmans, Hargroves, and Furloughs

Cary Reynolds's Steam Engine Dilemma

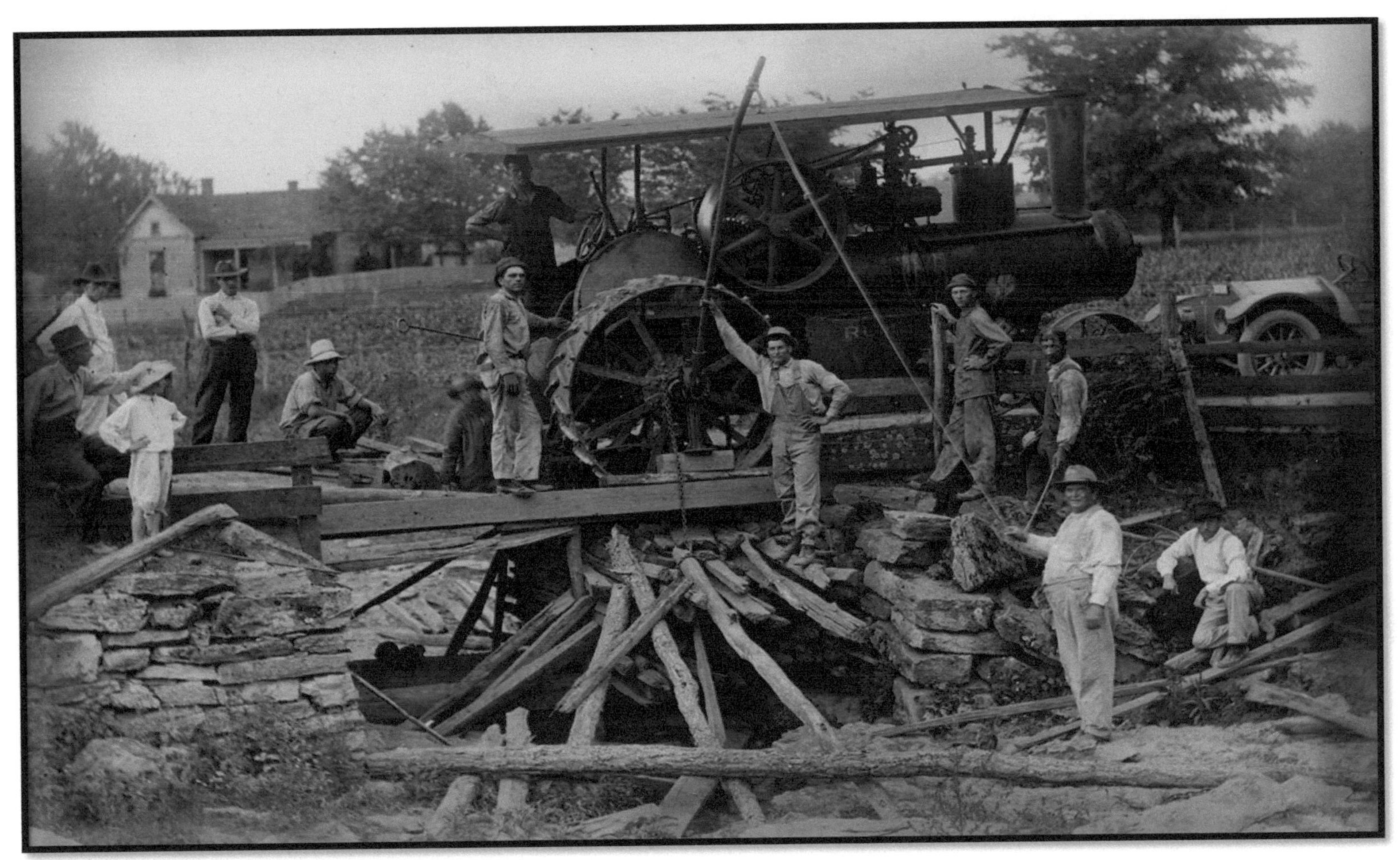

Cary Reynolds's steam engine collapsed the bridge on Old Hillsboro Road in 1918. Nan Rodgers Chapman's house is in the background. The stone abutments are still under Old Hillsboro Road.

Charlie Gray's Home in Bingham

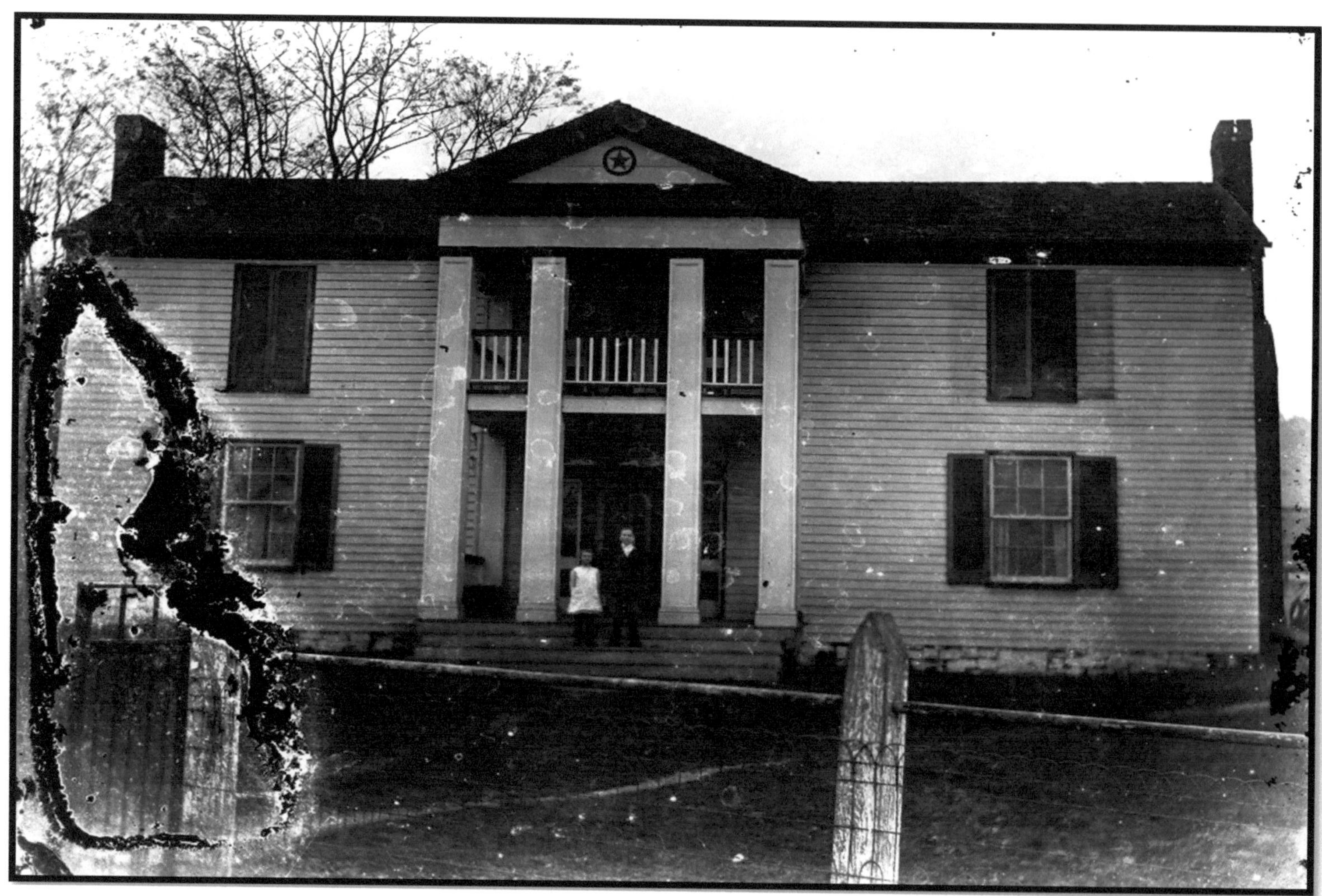

The home of Charlie Gray on Old Hillsboro Road was placed on the National Register of Historic Places in 1988. Little Margaret Gray and her cousin Dan Chapman pose for Mr. Parker. David and Elizabeth Lemke call it home today.

John Parker's Home in Bingham

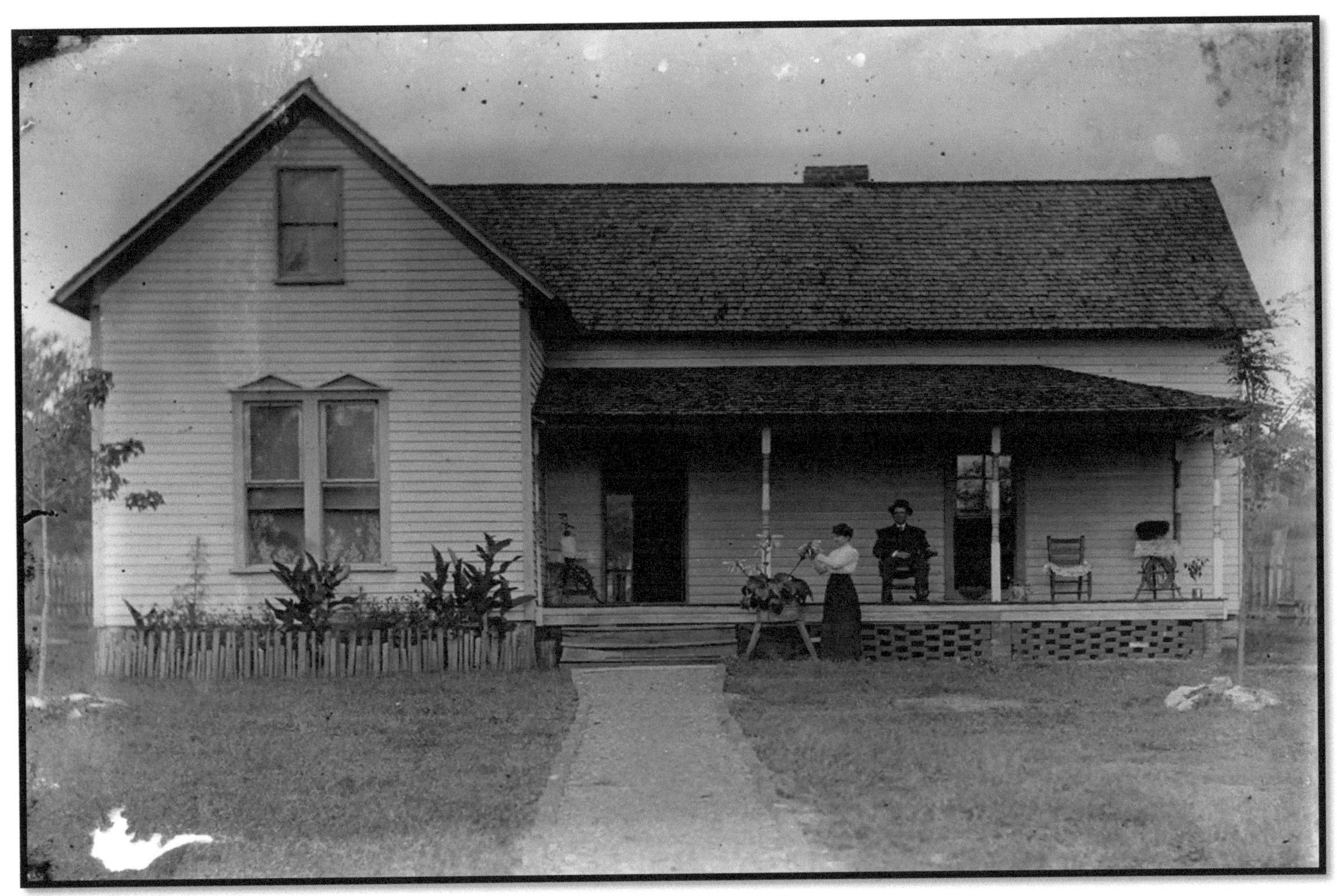

The home of John and Sadie Parker was on Parker Branch Road. Later, it became the home of Floyd and Mattie Dorton Vest. Sadly, it was torn down 2019, after years of being vacant.

Bingham's Version of Madonna and Child

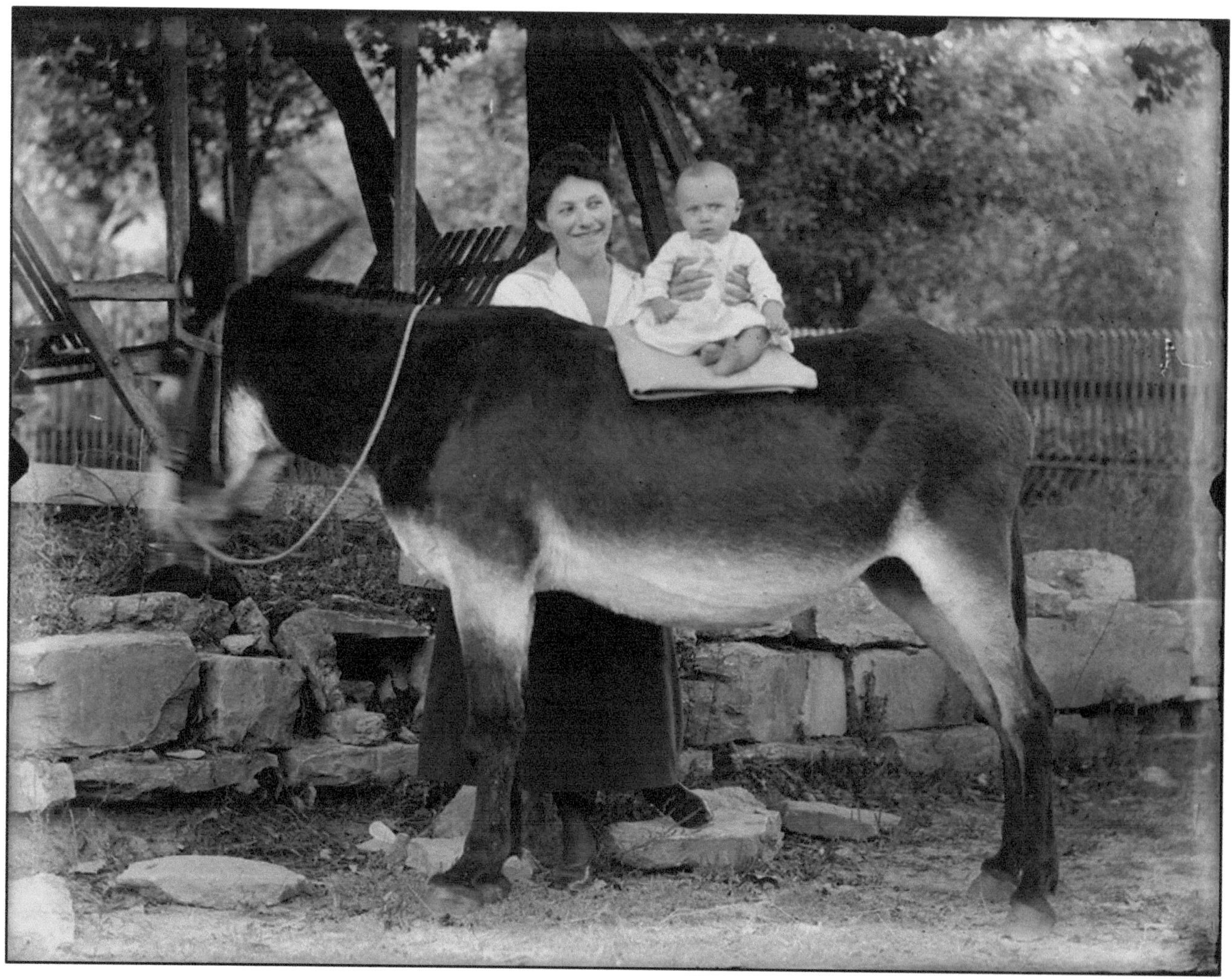

Unidentified mother and child with donkey in Parker's front yard.

Bingham Neighbors

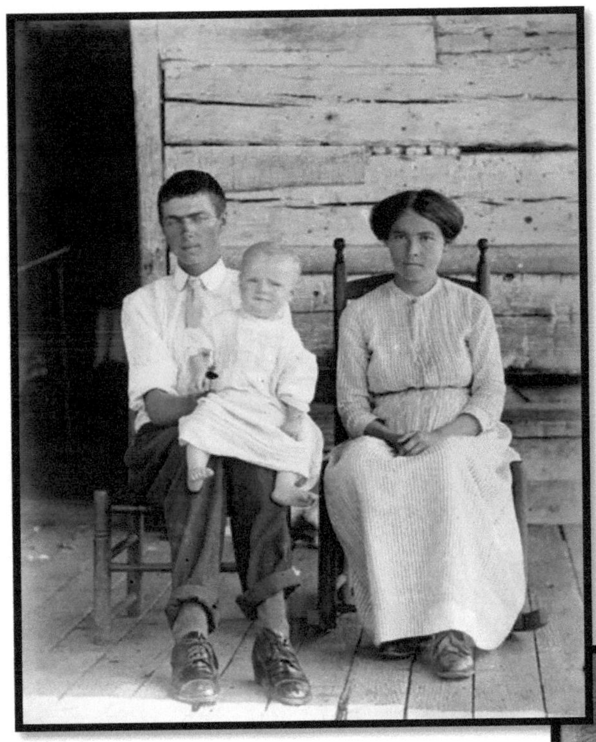

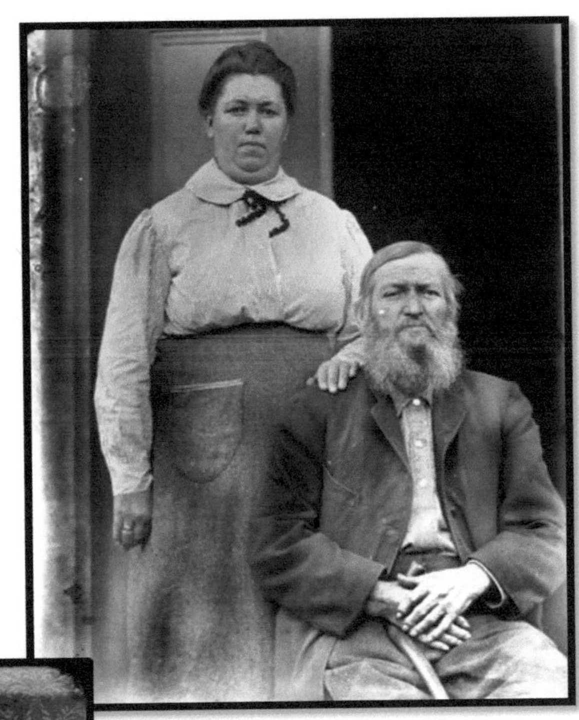

Matilda and Albert Speight lived on Old Charlotte Road.

→

Albert worked at the sawmill, according to the 1910 U.S. census.

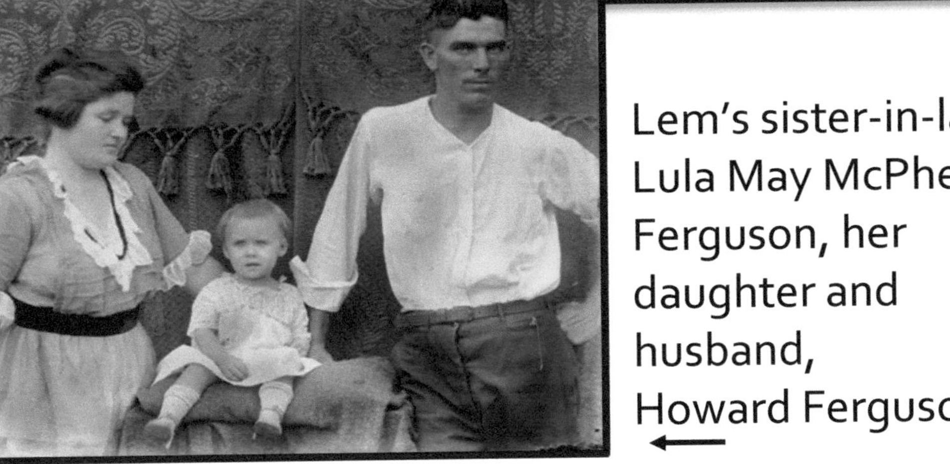

Leslie Logan, holding son, German, and Janie Wray Logan lived in a cabin in Parker's yard.

Lem's sister-in-law, Lula May McPherson Ferguson, her daughter and husband, Howard Ferguson.

←

Bingham Neighbors

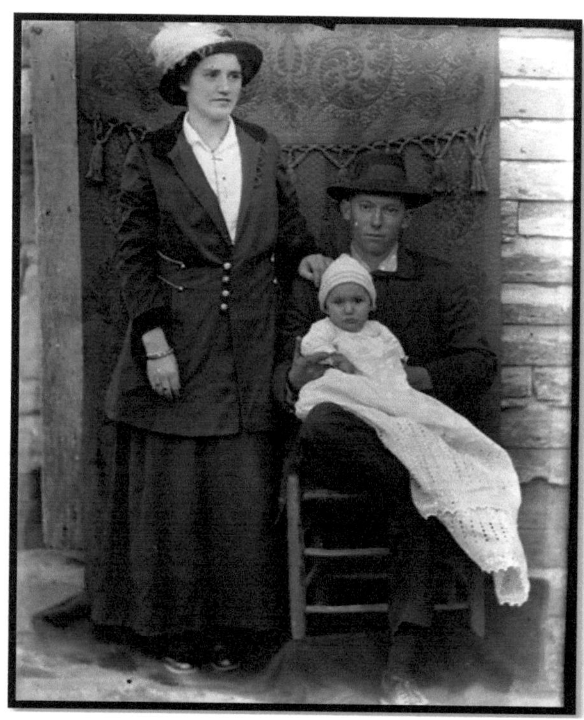

Joe and Myrtle Hester Mays and child were neighbors.

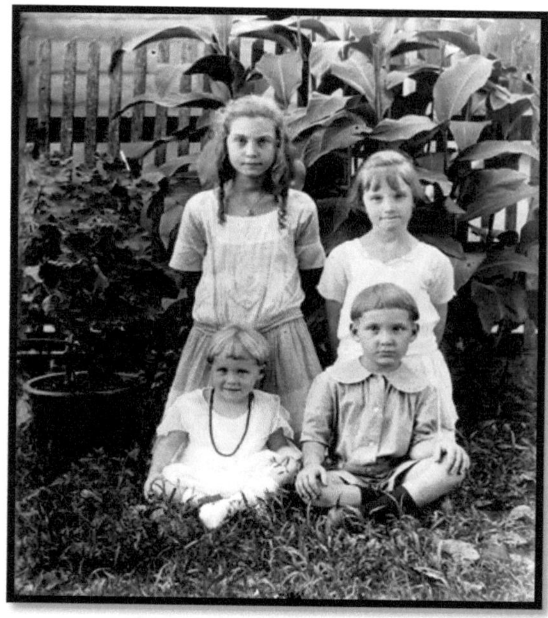

Harley Parker with female cousins

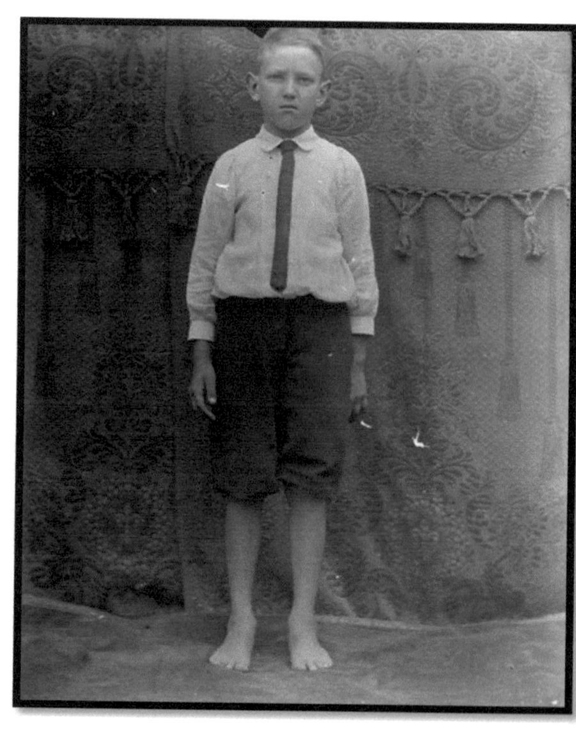

DeRay Reid lived next door to the Parkers.

Lemuel Parker Family

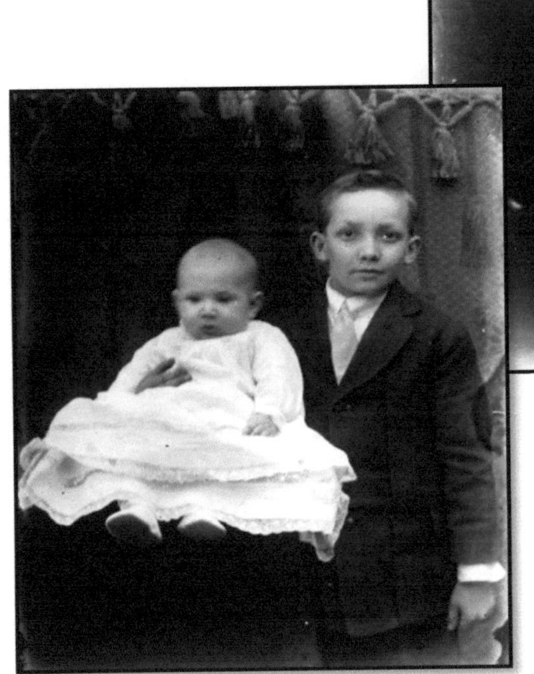

Harley and Millard

Millard, Harley, and Laura Parker,
in front row.
John Dorton, John and Sadie
Pentacost Parker, in back.

Millard and Harley

Bingham Neighbors

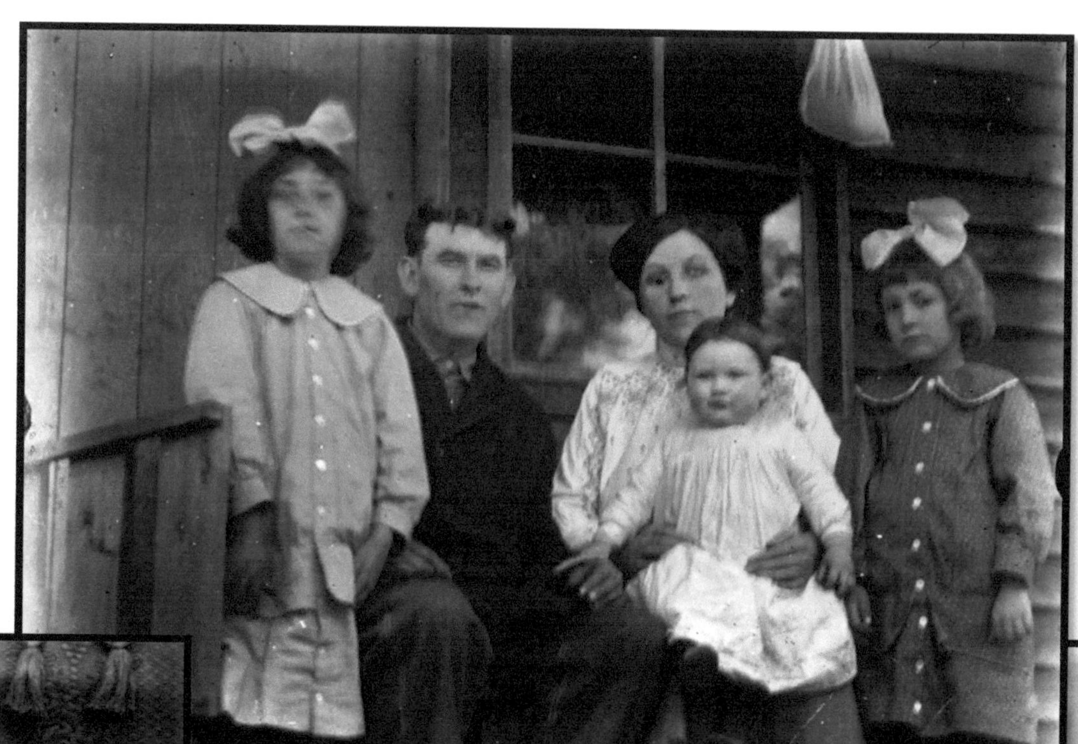

Above: unidentified family

Left: John Tucker's daughter

Right: Dr. Eddleman's daughter

Grandmother Parker and Great-Grandmother McPherson

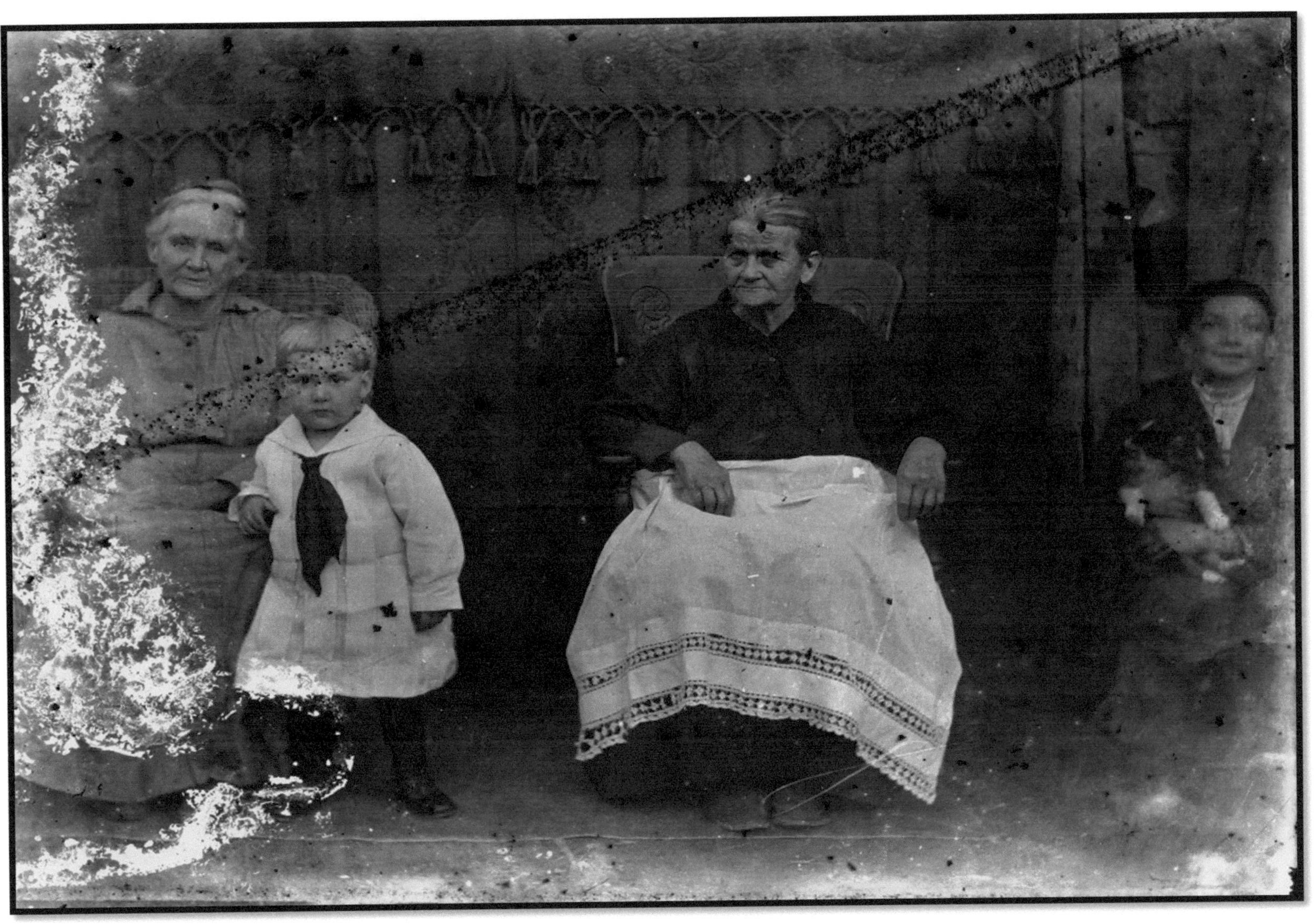

Amanda Bingham Parker, Harley, Eleanor Boyd McPherson, Millard

Lemuel Parker's In-Laws

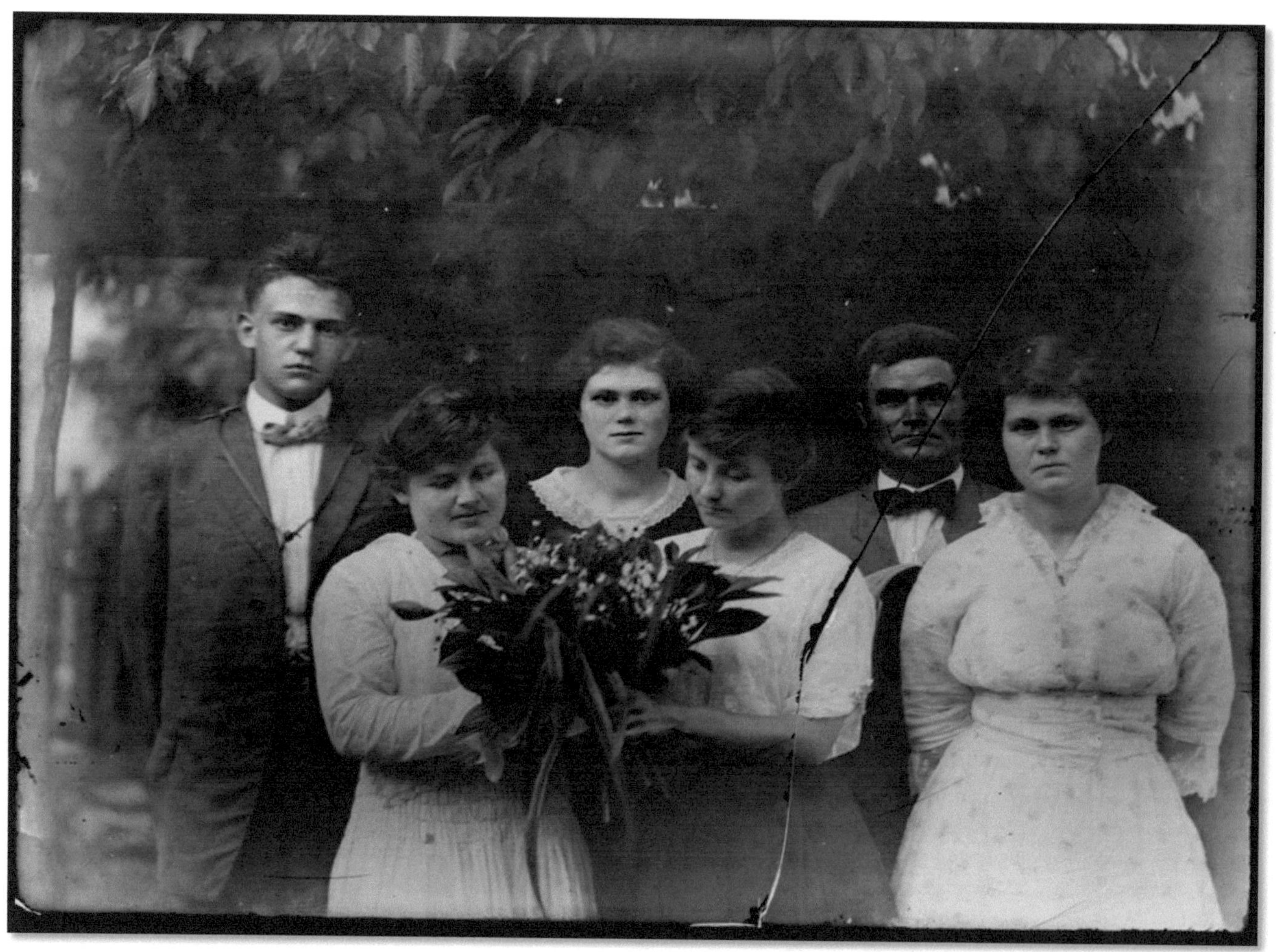

Hugh Smith, unidentified lady, Lena Grimes Smith,
Laura Parker, Green and Jenny Grimes McPherson

The Village of Leiper's Fork / Hillsboro

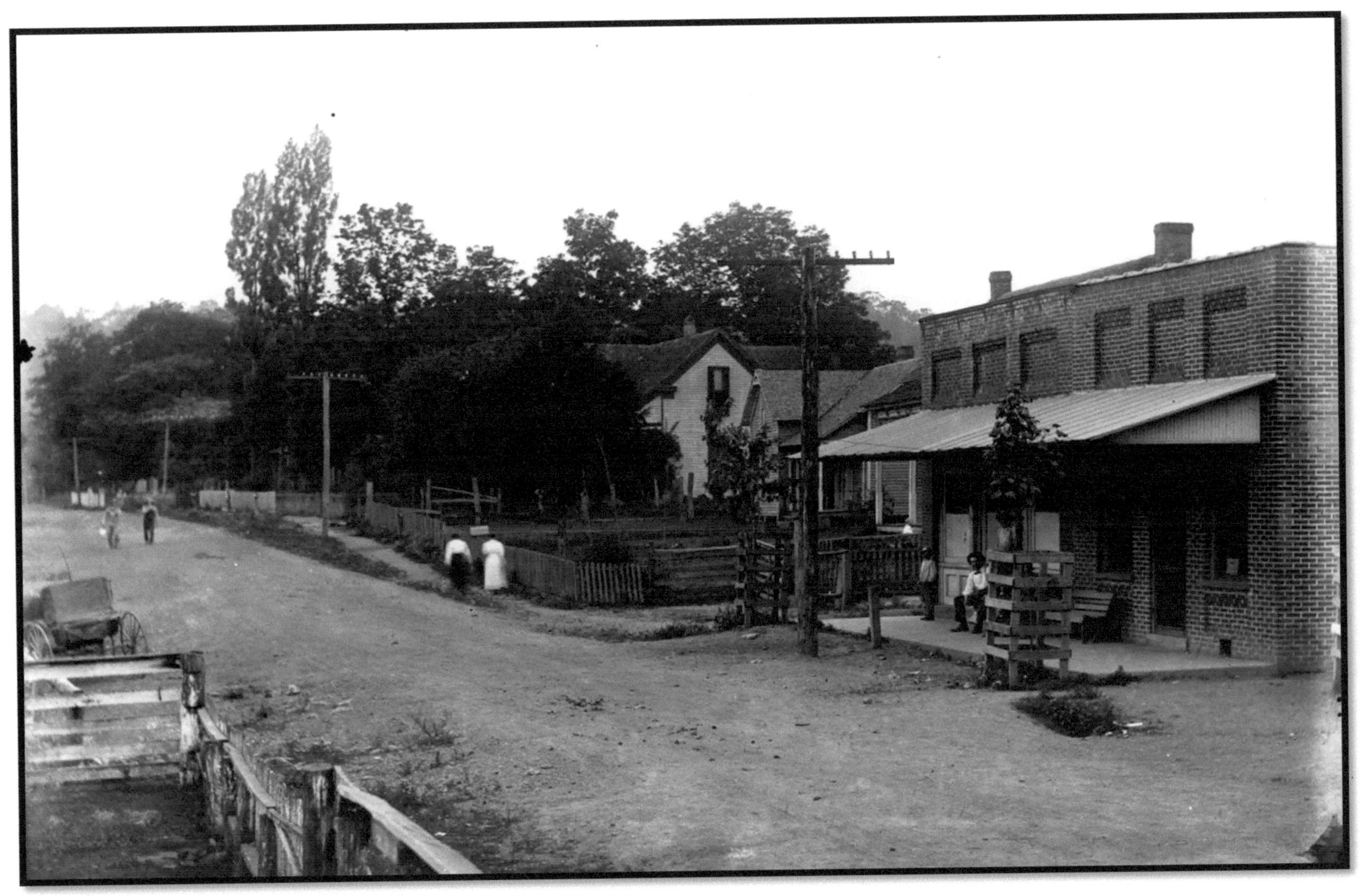

The Bank of Leiper's Fork (1911-1932) in the heart of the village. ca. 1915

The Village of Leiper's Fork / Hillsboro

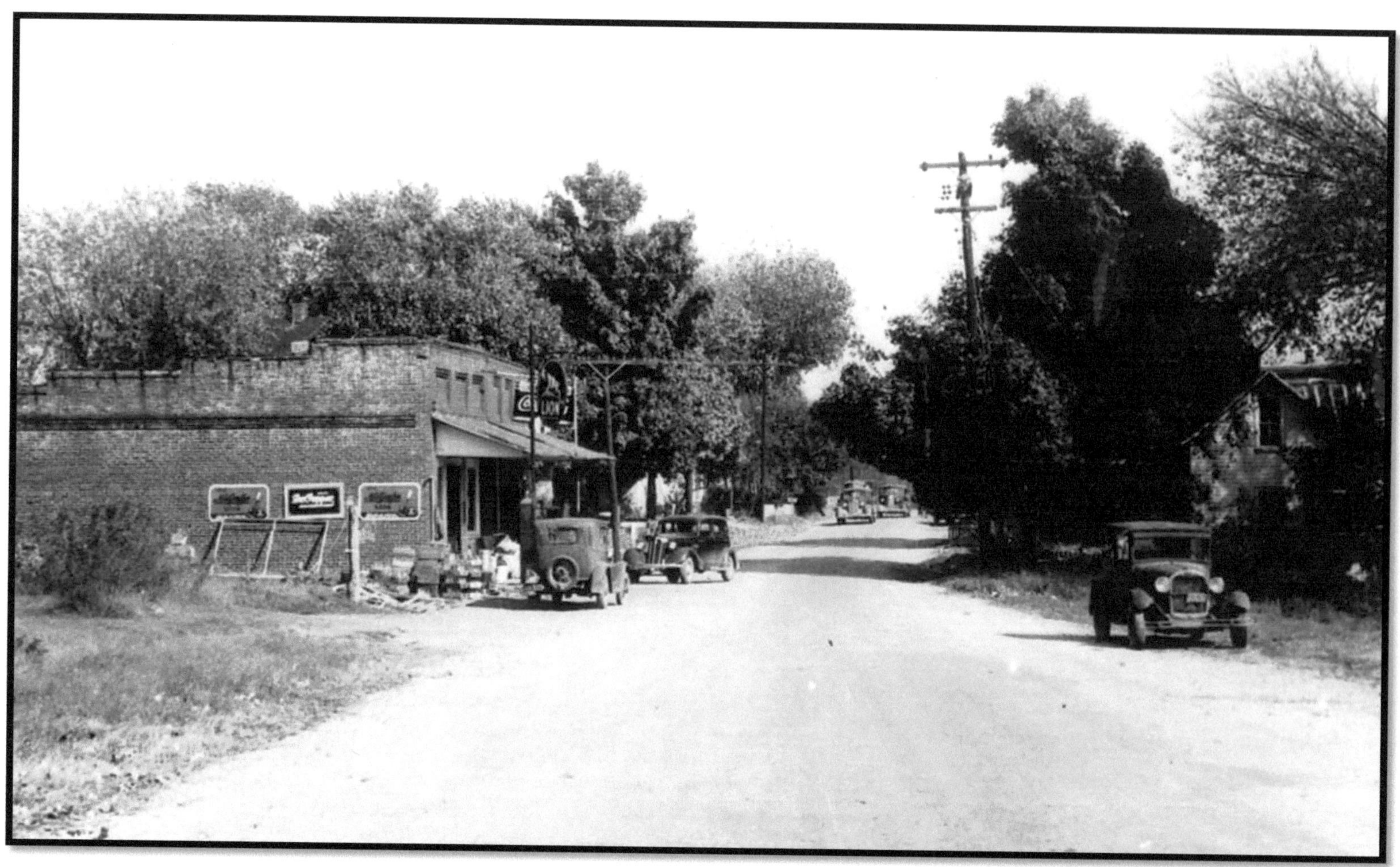

A nostalgic view of the village with Gus Carl's store and the Bank of Leiper's Fork on the left. Taken from the Church of Christ looking north.

J.W. Parham's Home and Store

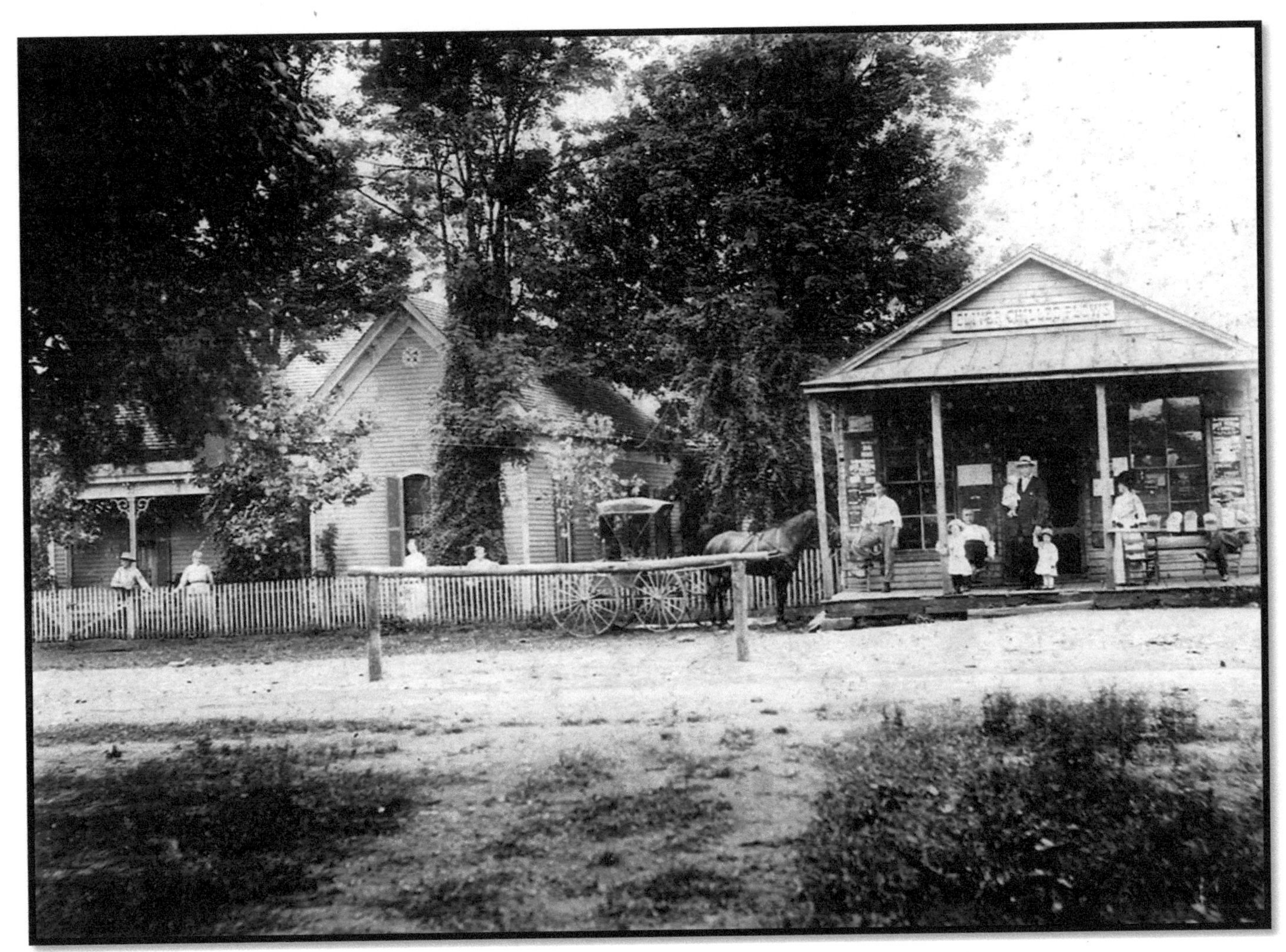

The Leiper's Fork Post-Office was inside Parham's Store. J. W., Virginia, Laura, and Bunyan Parham are standing at the picket fence. The village had a post-office from 1818 until 1918, except for a brief period in the 1860s.

The Village of Leiper's Fork / Hillsboro

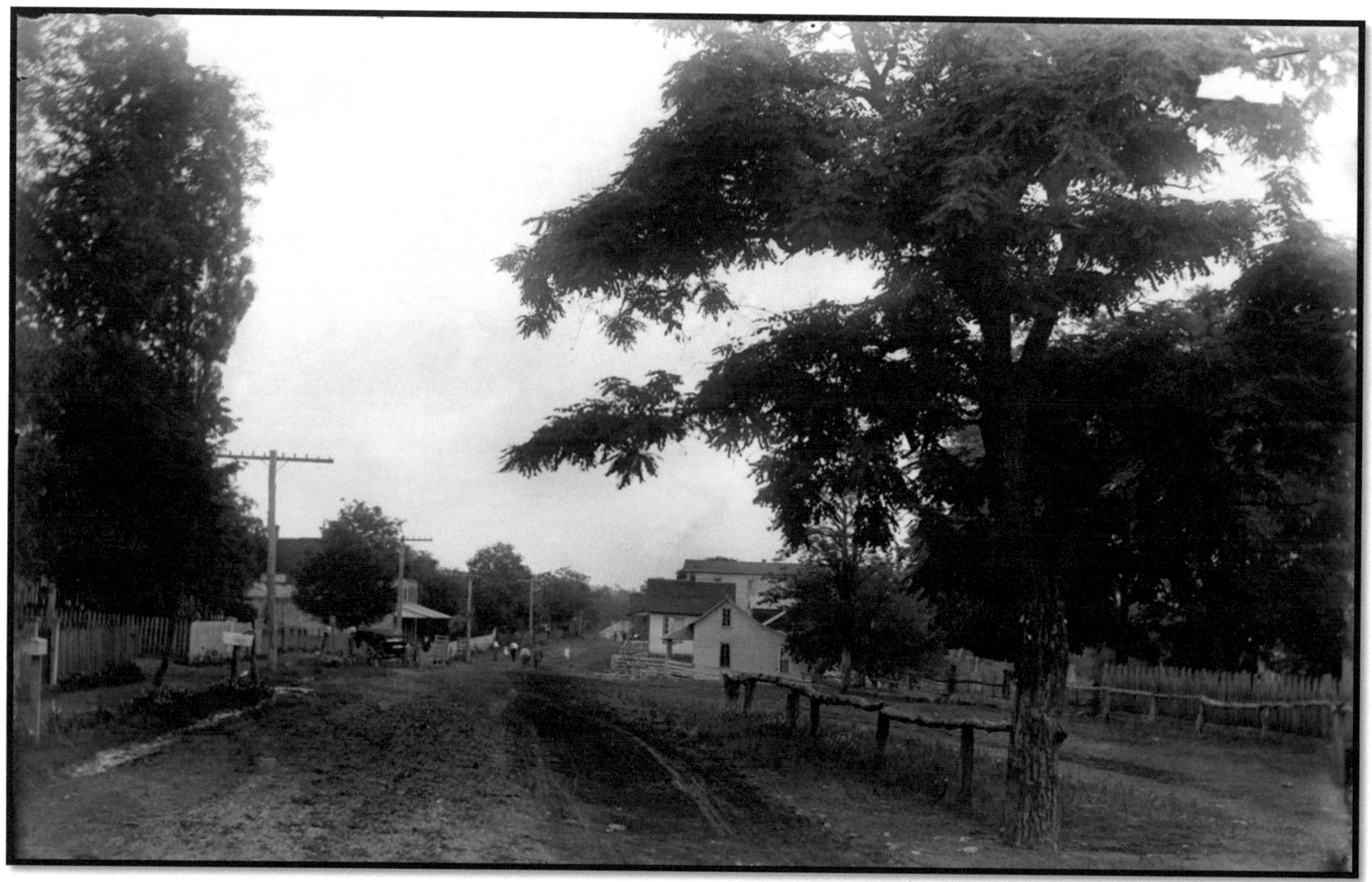

The village of Leiper's Fork ca. 1916, looking north, as seen from in front of the Church of Christ. The Bank of Leiper's Fork may be seen on the left and Dr. N. M. Tucker's office is on the right. The horse-rails secured the horses while families attended church.

Joseph L. Sweeney — Village Blacksmith

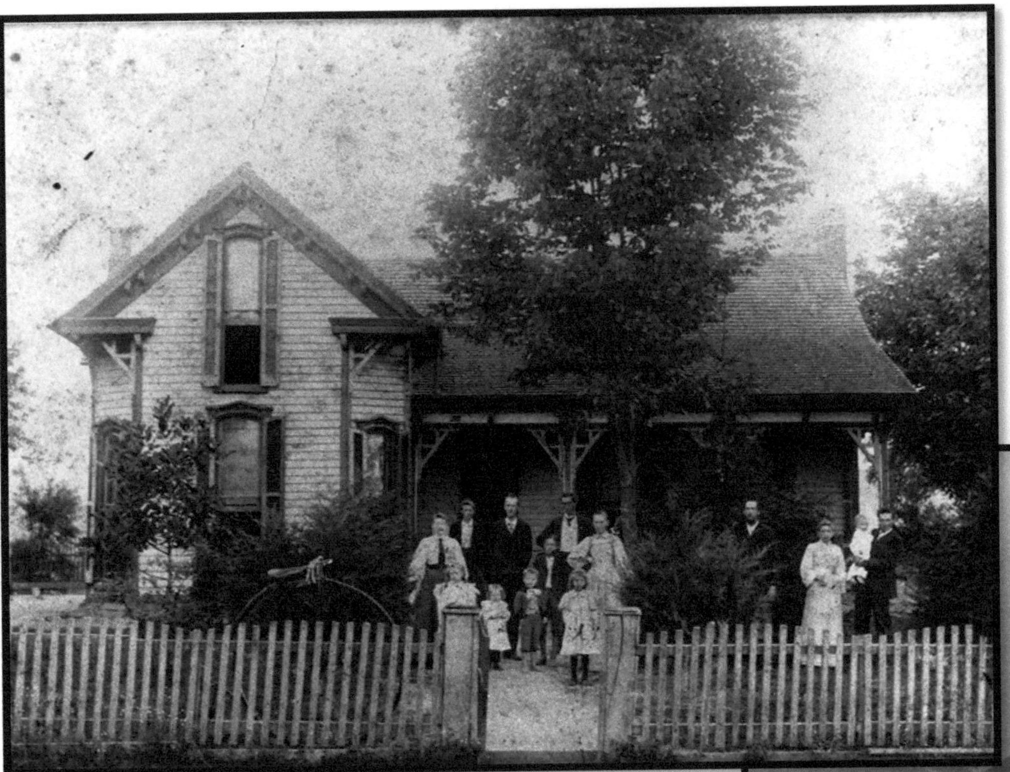

J. L. and Minerva Gatlin Sweeney were the parents of 13 children and lived in this house he built in 1879. The Church of Christ was across the road, to which they were all dedicated members. ←

Joseph L. Sweeney proudly exhibits his patent (Sept 30, 1913) on this wagon bed. He was also a skilled blacksmith and a CSA veteran. →

The Village Blacksmith and Wagonmaker

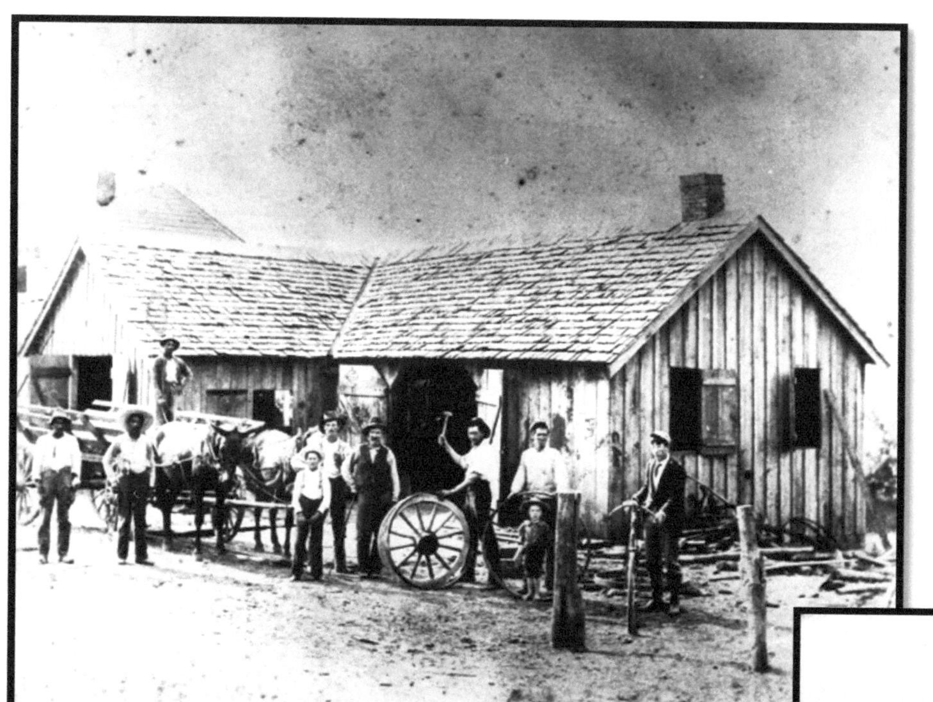

J. L. Sweeney's blacksmith shop was located across from the Leiper's Fork Bank and next to the Church of Christ. Being in the middle of the village, it was a great place to gather for local news and gossip.

←

J. L. Sweeney's patented wagon bed was popular with farmers for its adjustable sides, which could haul loose hay with the sides down or corn with the sides up. ⟶

J. T. Sweeney — Another Village Blacksmith

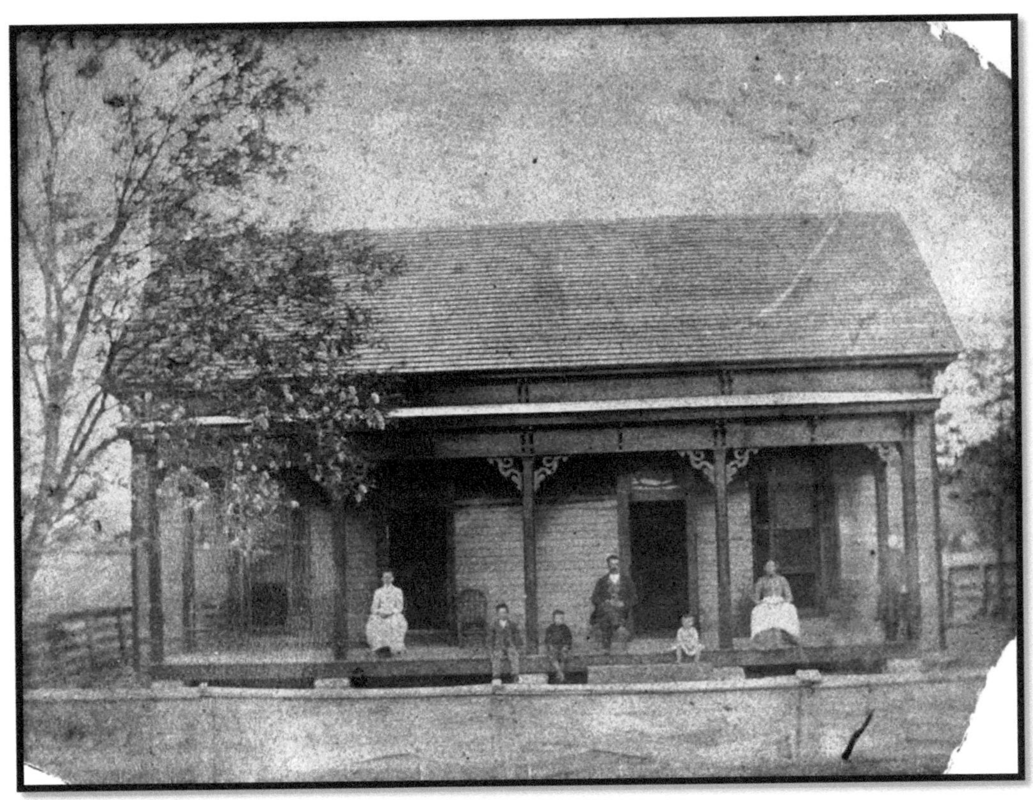

The J. T. Sweeney home was located where Leiper's Fork Art Gallery is today. J. T. Sweeney followed his Uncle J. L.'s trade but on a smaller scale.

J. T. Sweeney's blacksmith shop, later J. M. Inman's, was located where Fox & Locke is today.

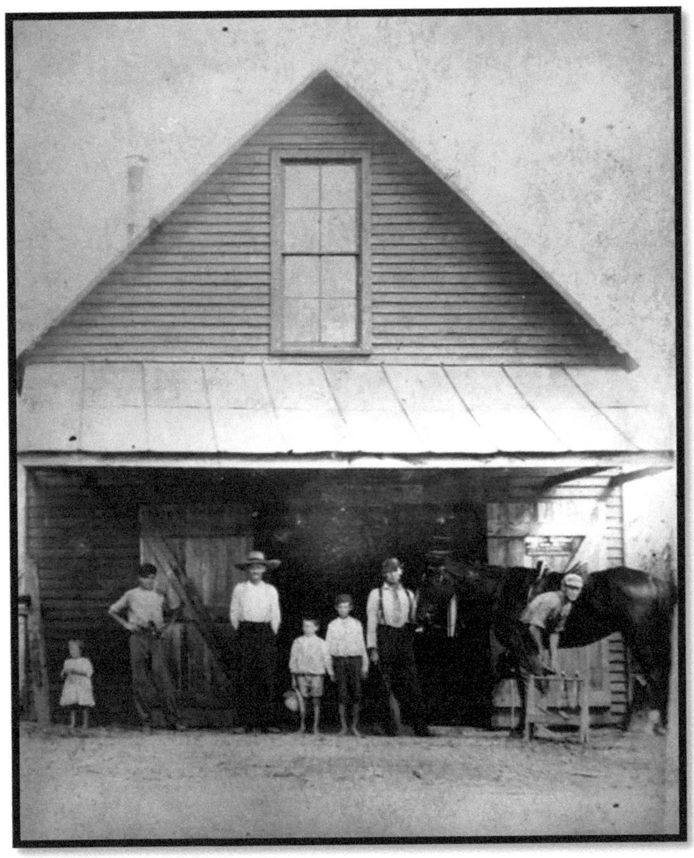

The Village Doctor

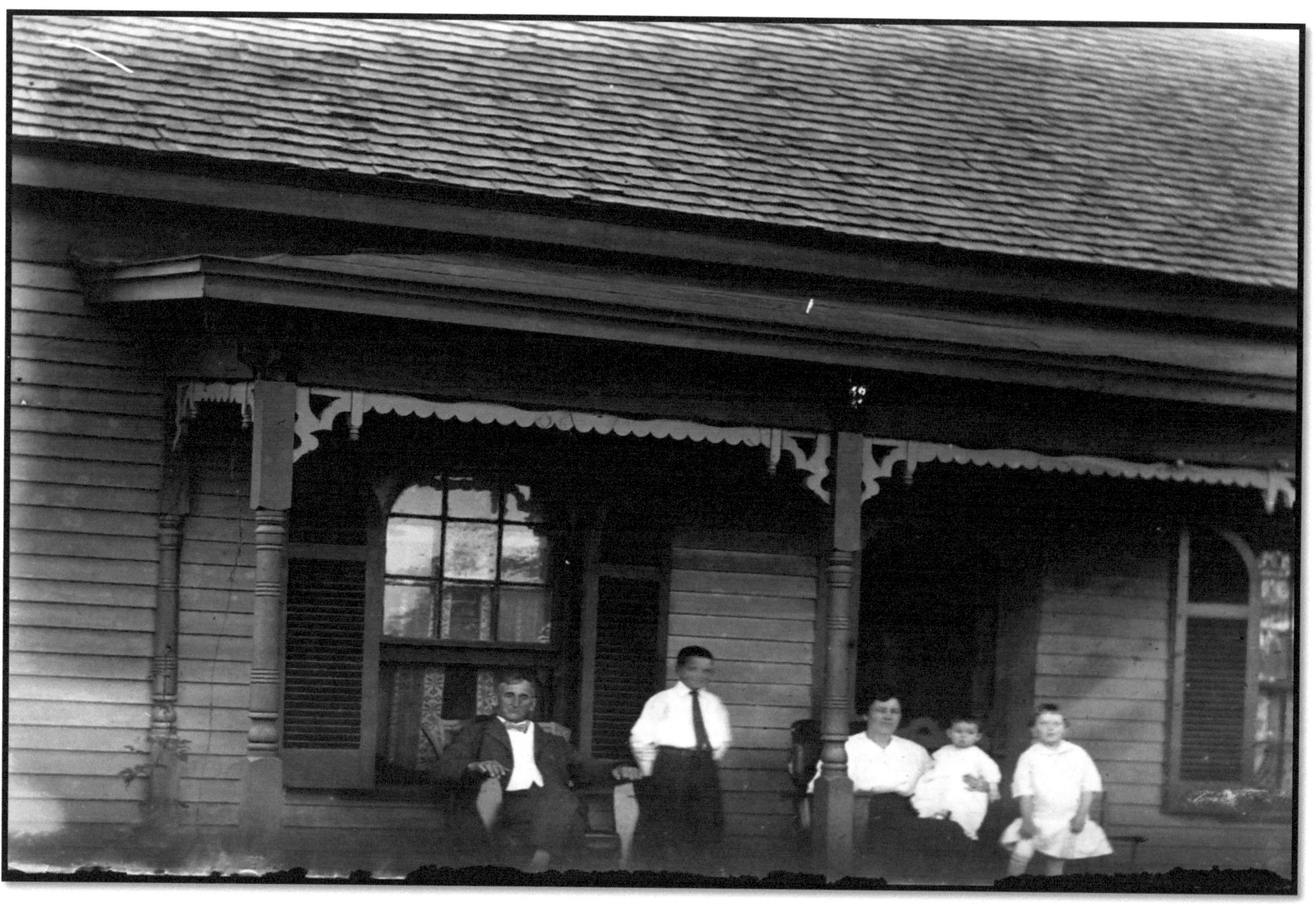

Dr. John M. Drake and family — Mack, Bessie, Millard, Hazel.

Another Village Doctor

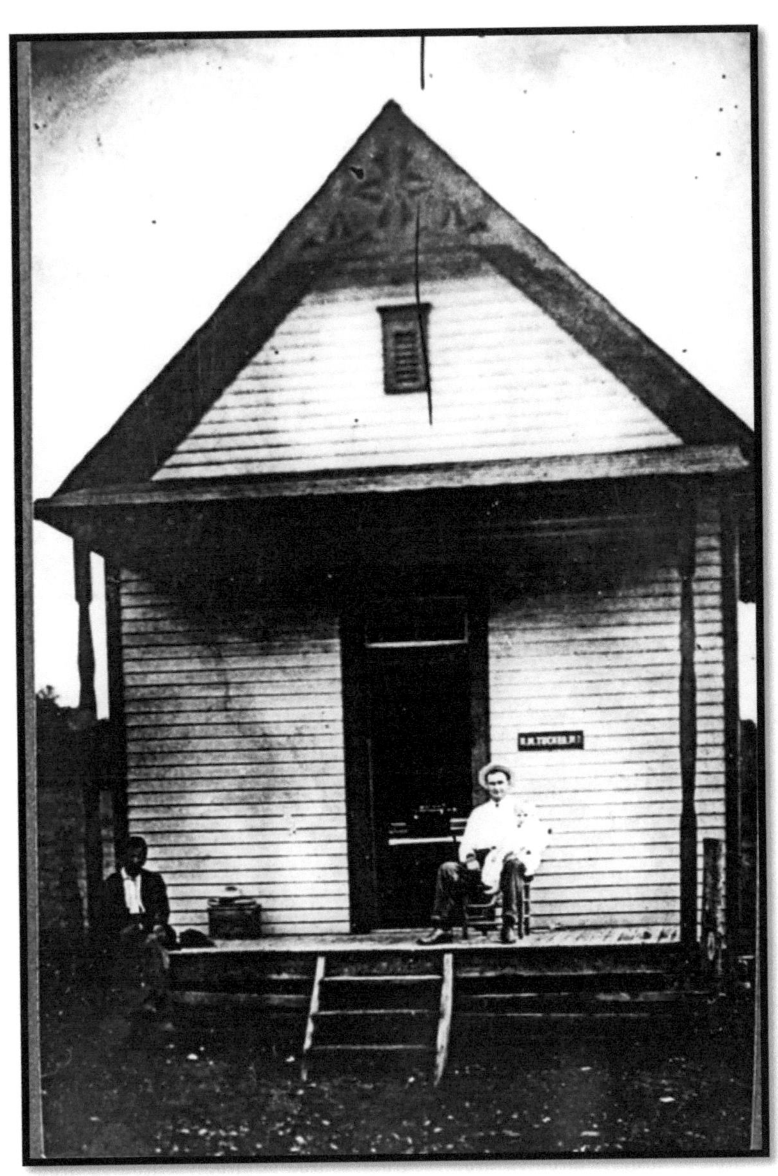

Dr. N. M. Tucker came to Leiper's Fork in 1906 and purchased the two-story house on the corner leading to Hillsboro School and the Methodist Church. He purchased the music room from the school, moved it across the road from his house and made it his office. Seen here with his daughter in front of his office, Dr. Tucker enjoyed a wide practice in the community and surrounding countryside.

Village Houses of Worship

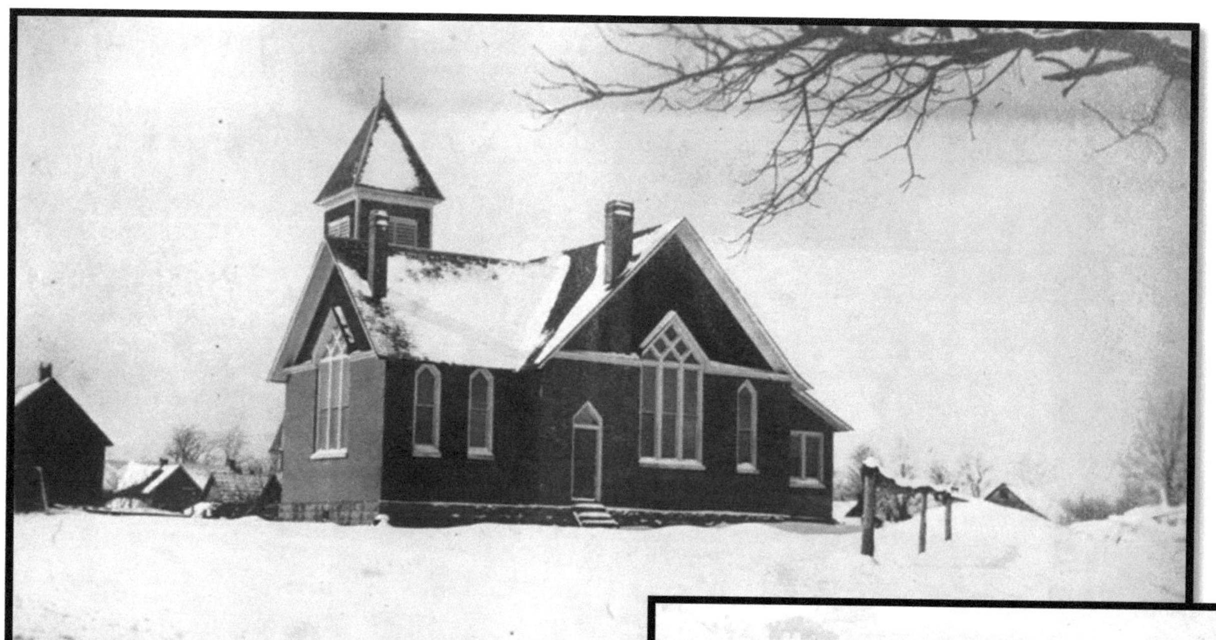

Hillsboro Methodist Church, built in 1911, has an active congregation ←

Leiper's Fork Church of Christ was organized in 1831. This building was built in 1876 and stands today in the center of the village. J. W. Parham's home and store can be seen in the background. →

Southall Brothers Sawmill

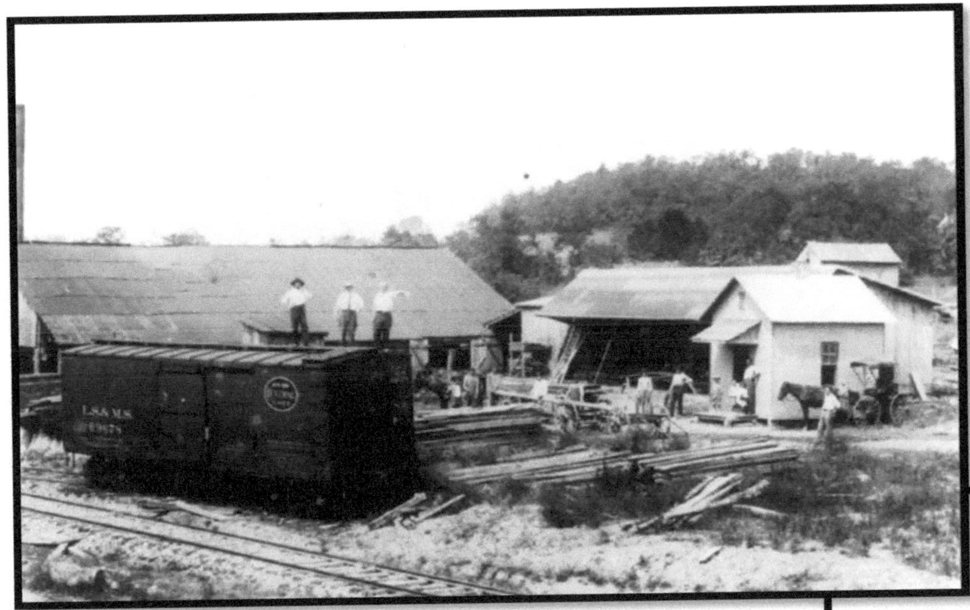

Southall Brothers Sawmill was the largest business in Leiper's Fork, shipping a large volume of hardwood lumber on the M.T.R.R. Many local houses were built with Southall lumber.

The Middle Tennessee Railroad came to Leiper's Fork in 1909. The train ran from Franklin to Mt. Pleasant twice daily until 1927. The depot may be seen on the left.

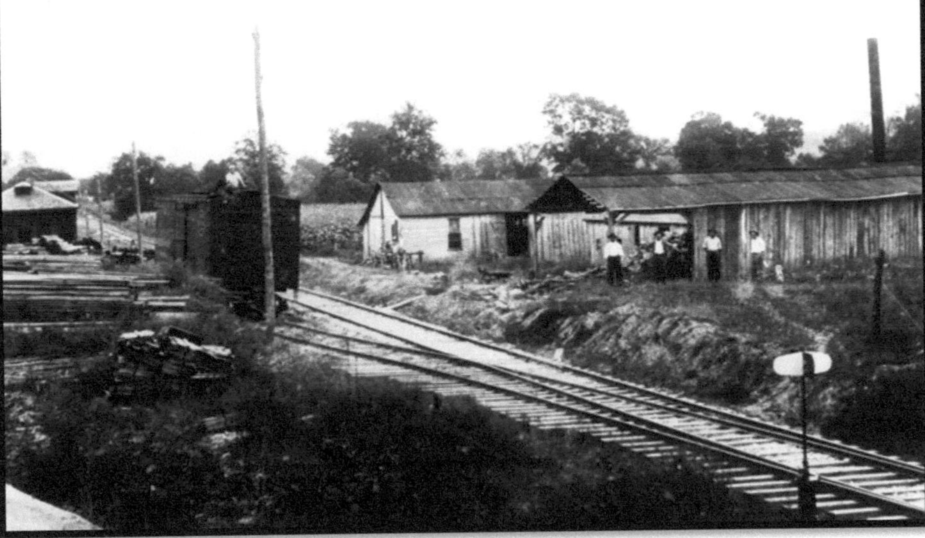

Middle Tennessee Railroad Depot

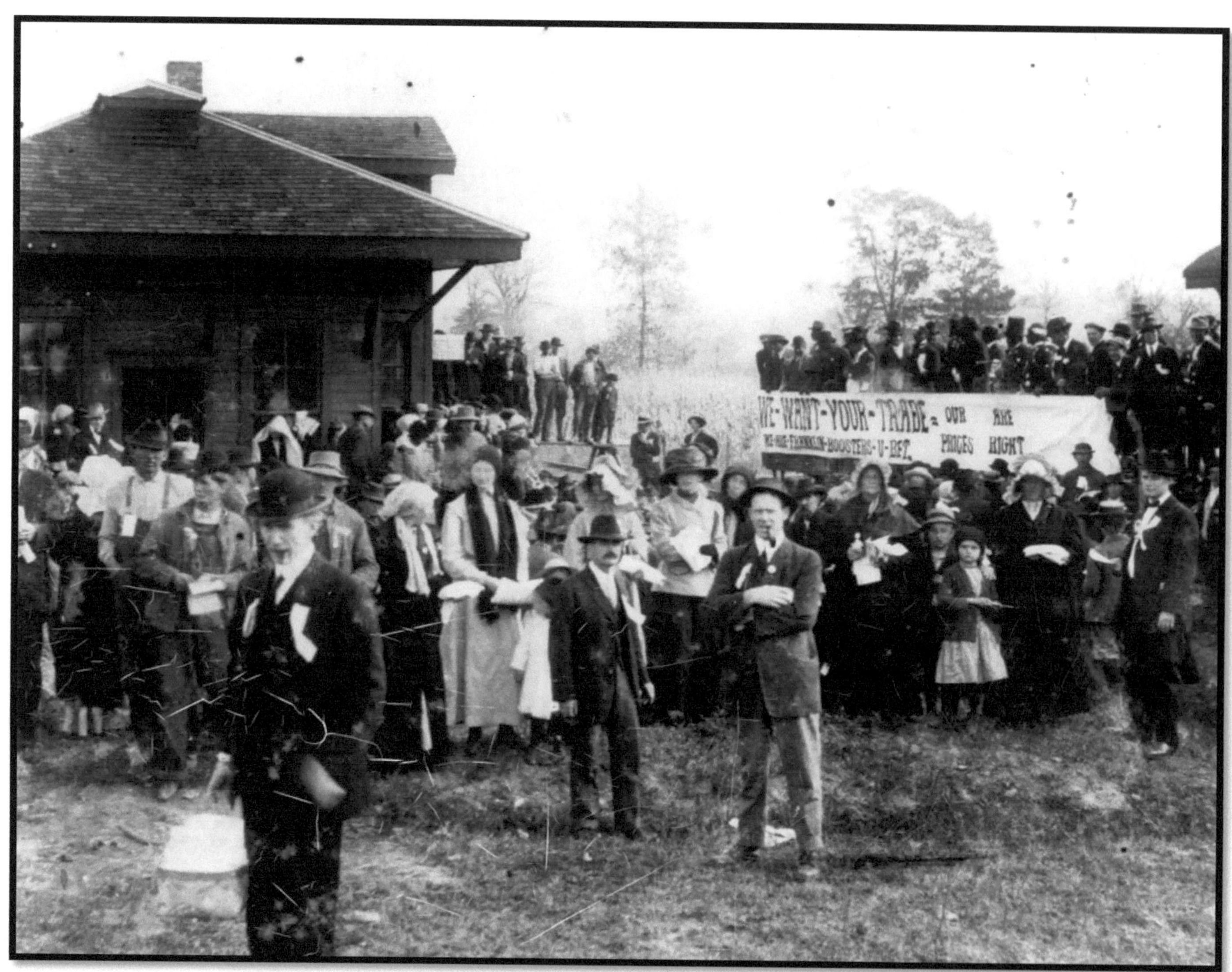

In 1921, the Franklin Boosters came to the Leiper's Fork Depot

Benton Heights — Home of W. L. Pinkerton

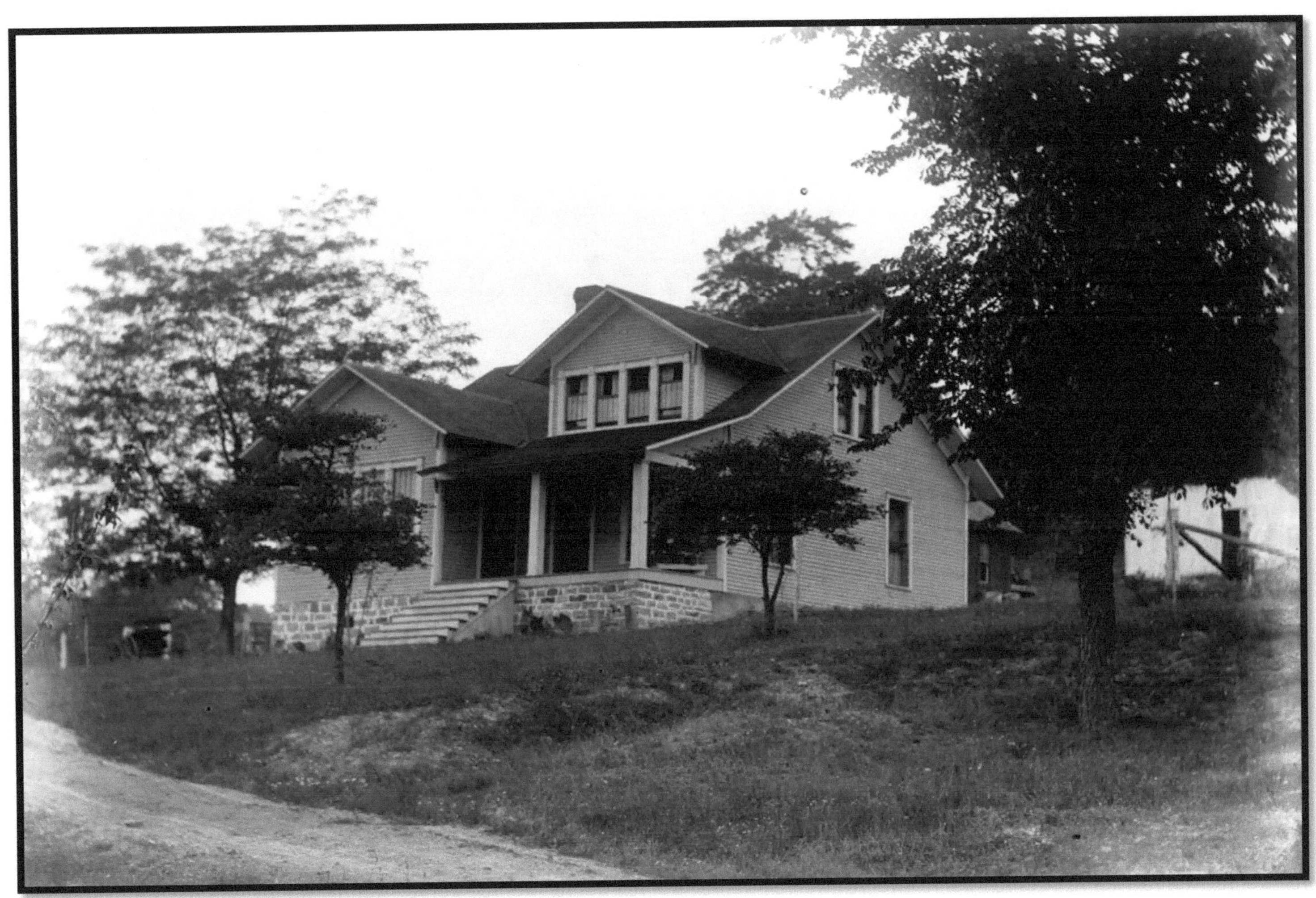

Benton Heights, built in 1910, was the home of W. L. Pinkerton, cashier of the Bank of Leiper's Fork, and later, the home of Richard and Florence Pigue. Lastly, the home of Henry and Lura Davis before it burned in 1936.

The Home of Clint Shaw, Rural Mail Carrier

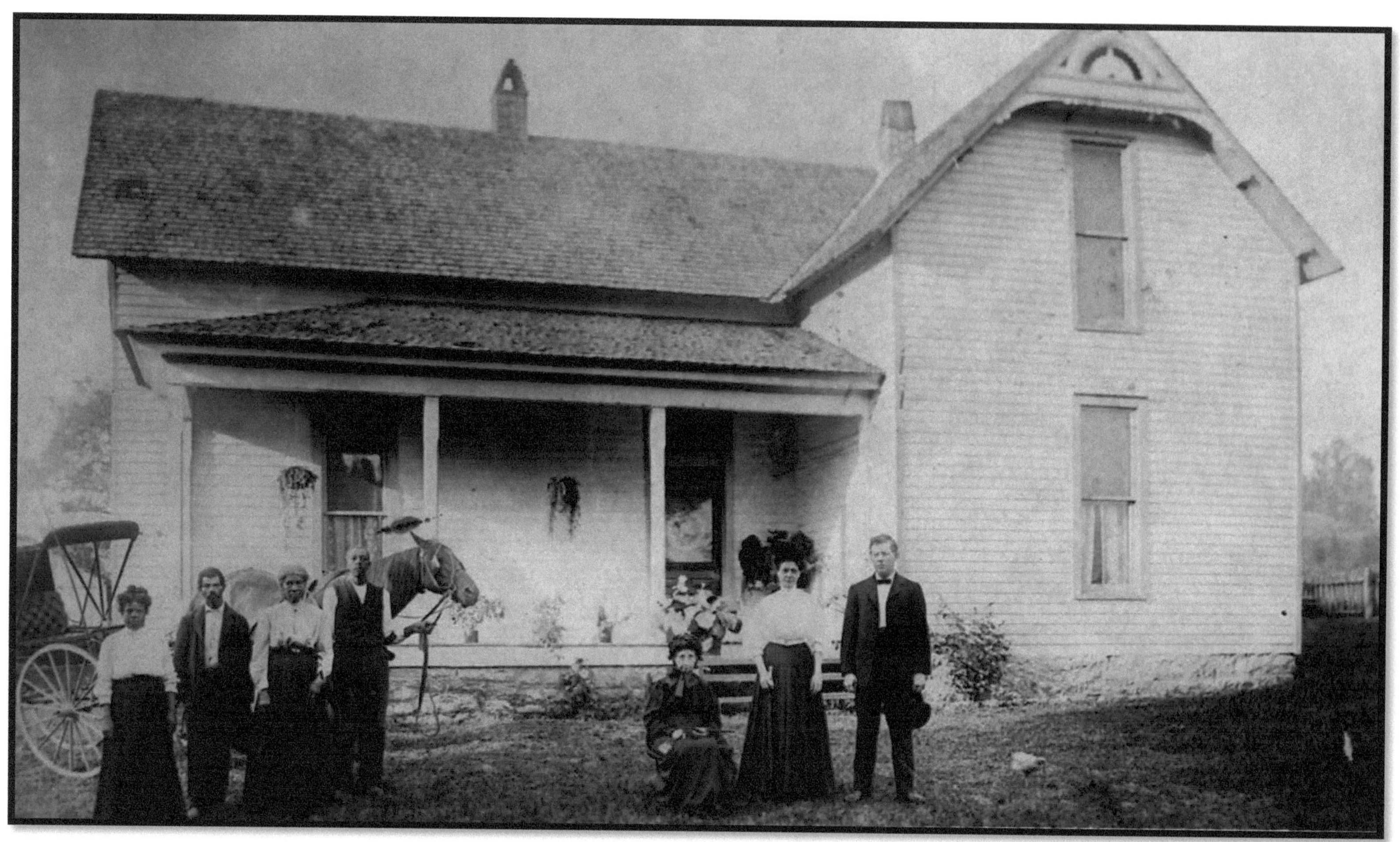

The Lizzie Walker family lived across Bailey Road from the Clint Shaw family. Mrs. Emily Sparkman Prowell sits with her black bonnet and dress still in mourning for her husband. Clint Shaw used the buggy to deliver the mail for Rural Route 6.

Rest in Peace

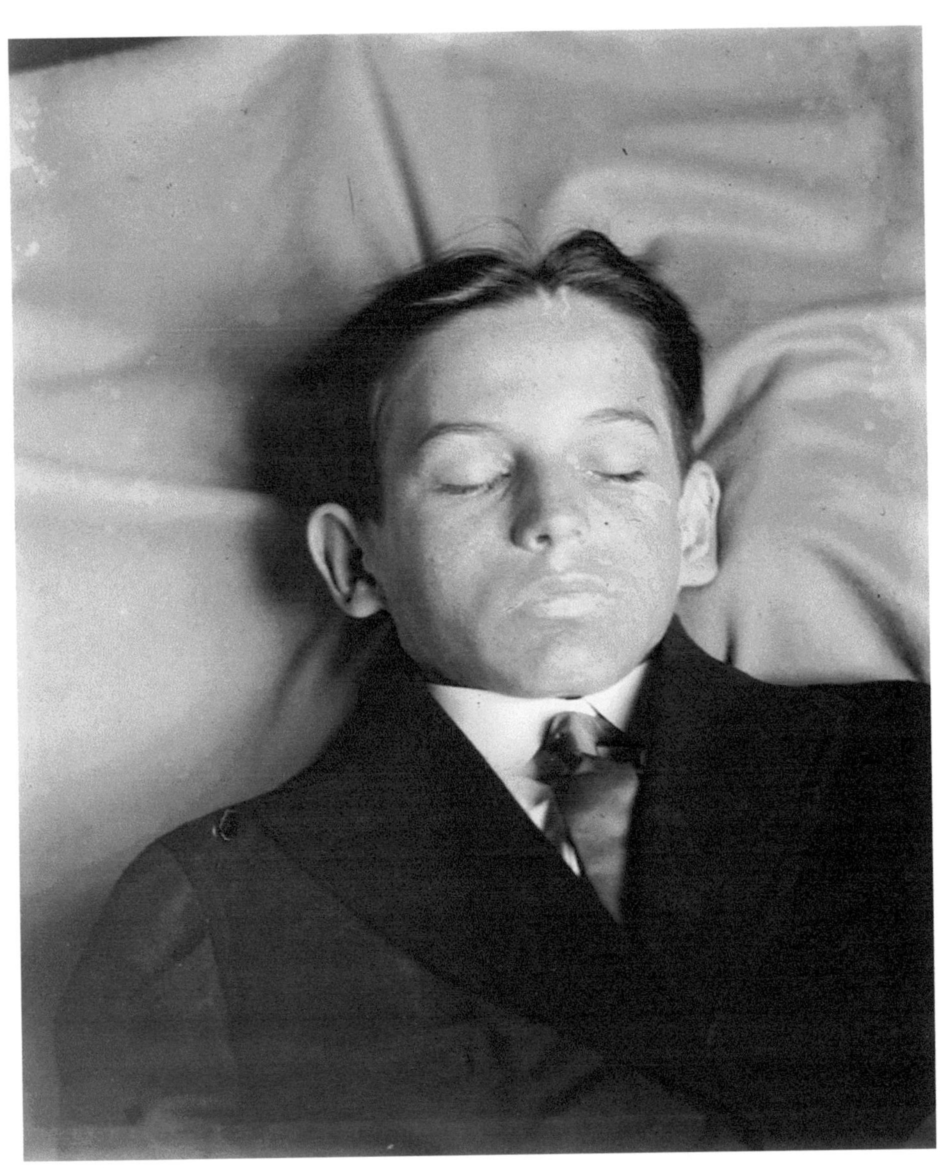

Herman Martin (1899-1915), son of W. T. Martin, is buried in the Leiper's Fork Cemetery.

Heads Up! The End.

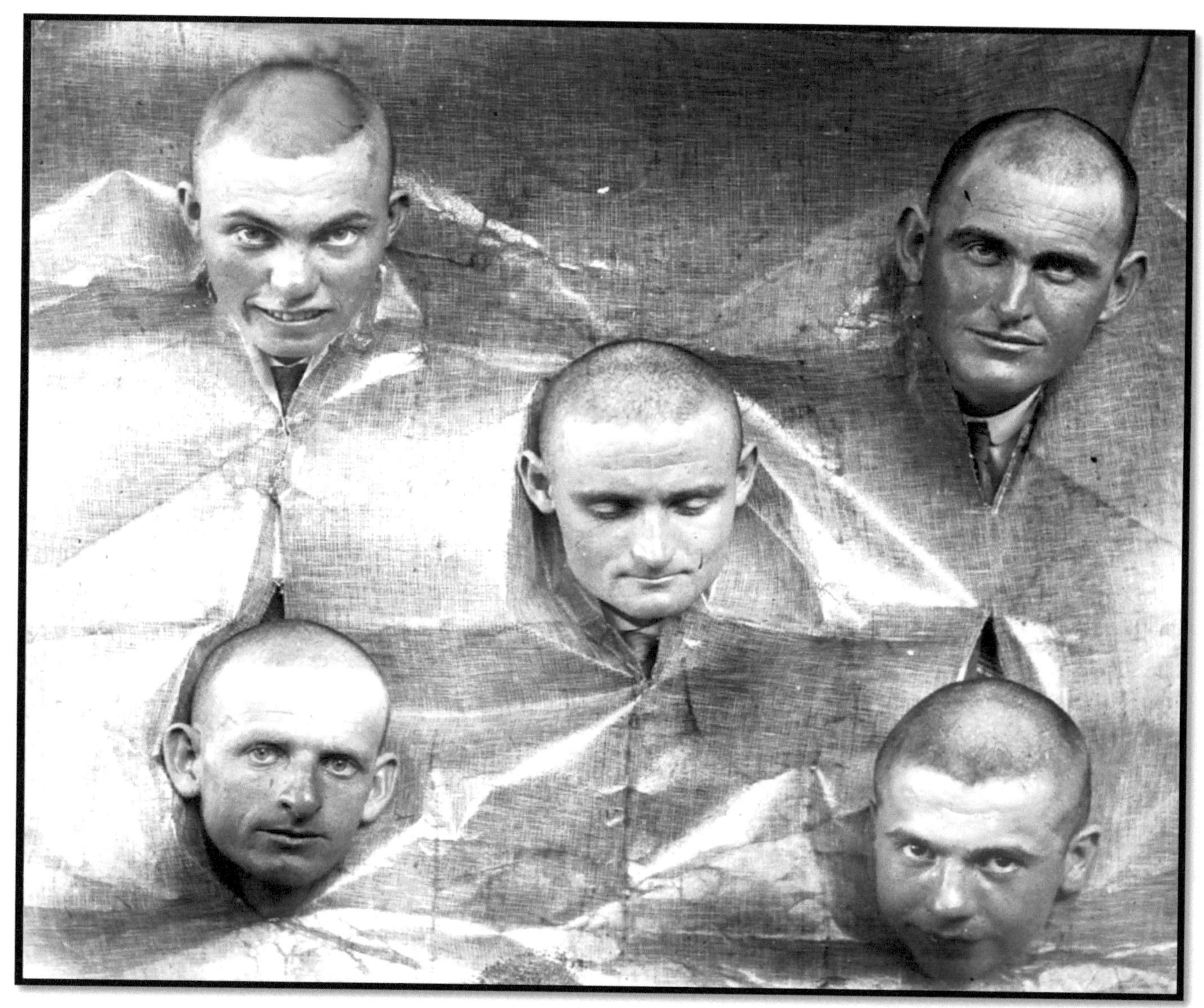

Bingham buddies with buzz-haircuts, possibly after joining the army in 1917.